A Monarch Americana Book

King Of The Harem Heaven

*The Amazing True Story Of A Daring Charlatan
Who Ran A Virgin Love Cult in America*

Anthony Sterling

"Beware of false prophets,
which come to you in sheep's clothing,
but inwardly they are ravening wolves."

Matthew 7:15

MONARCH BOOKS, INC.

Derby, Connecticut

KING OF THE HAREM HEAVEN

A Monarch Americana Book
Published in January, 1960

Copyright © 1960 by Anthony Sterling

Nothing in this book is intended to reflect any discredit or obloquy on the reconstructed House of David or Israelite organization which, as far as the author and publisher know, presently fully conform to all the moral and legal principles of the communities in which they live.

Monarch Books are published by MONARCH BOOKS, INC., Capital Building, Derby, Connecticut, and represent the works of outstanding novelists and writers of non-fiction, especially chosen for their literary merit and reading entertainment.

A NIGHTHAWK BOOK REPRINT EDITION
Complete and Unabridged

Printed in the United States of America

ISBN: 979-8869144966

I AM THE LAW!

"*I am the new Messiah,*" he said, and people flocked to his side for salvation.

"*Give up your worldly goods,*" he thundered, and they poured their lifetime savings into his secret coffers.

"*Suffering is good for the soul,*" he told them, and they turned over their pay checks and ate sparingly while "The King" feasted.

"*I proclaim the Virgin Law,*" he announced, and husbands and wives lived as brothers and sisters.

"*Give me your girls for purification,*" he ordered, and parents offered up their teen-age daughters for his gratification.

This was Ben Purnell, King of the House of David, self-styled Redeemer and daring charlatan, who blazed a trail of licentiousness and debauchery across the State of Michigan.

AUTHOR'S PROFILE

Anthony Sterling is the pseudonym of a well-known writer and historian whose work has appeared regularly in THE SATURDAY EVENING POST, COSMOPOLITAN, THE VIRGINIA QUARTERLY REVIEW, ARGOSY and many other leading magazines, and whose books have repeatedly won critical acclaim. A life-long Michigan resident, he has blended numerous personal sources with intensive on-the-scene research in producing the first full-length account of the incredible life of King Ben Purnell.

CURRENT BESTSELLING MONARCH BOOKS

MB501 WOMEN IN TROUBLE as told to James Donner   35c
The truth about abortion in America. With more than 40 case histories. A Monarch Human Behavior Book.

MB502 THE SEXUAL SIDE OF LIFE by Don James   35c
A frank, revealing study of love and sex in modern society. A Monarch Human Behavior Book.

MB503 TORMENTED WOMEN by Edward J. McGoldrick, Jr.   35c
A realistic commentary about women degraded and ravaged by alcohol. A Monarch Human Behavior Book.

MA300 KING OF THE HAREM HEAVEN by Anthony Sterling   35c
The true story of a daring charlatan who ran a virgin love cult in America. First title in the new Monarch Americana Series.

117 STRONGER THAN PASSION (The Piper's Tune) by George Byram   35c
122 SEASON FOR LOVE by Whitman Chambers   35c
124 ALL I CAN GET by William Ard   35c
125 NIKKI by Stuart Friedman   35c
127 LUST TO LIVE by Peter W. Denzer   35c
129 END TO INNOCENCE by Robert Carse   35c
132 SAVE THEM FOR VIOLENCE by James M. Fox   35c
133 THE FLESH PEDDLERS by Frank Boyd   35c
137 JAILBAIT STREET by Hal Ellson   35c
138 STEPHANA by Joseph Foster   35c
139 IN SAVAGE SURRENDER by Whitman Chambers   35c
140 THE GLORY JUMPERS by Delano Stagg   35c
141 FALCONS OF FRANCE by Charles Nordhoff and James Norman Hall 35c
142 NIGHT AFTER NIGHT by Steve Thurman   35c
143 JACK THE RIPPER by Stuart James   35c
A compelling novel about the shocking exploits of Jack The Ripper, based on the current Joseph E. Levine motion picture.

144 THE REVOLT OF JILL BRADDOCK by Stuart Friedman   35c

Available at all newsstands and bookstores

If you are unable to secure these books at your local dealer, you may obtain copies by sending the retail price plus 5c for handling each title to Monarch Books, Inc., Mail Order Department, Division Street, Derby, Connecticut.

INTRODUCTION

Early in 1958, the Michigan Department of Conservation announced that it was purchasing lonely little High Island in Upper Lake Michigan for use as a wildlife study area, a breeding ground for grouse. If you'd fished those waters and gone ashore there, you'd have found the rotting ruins of a single building and traces of the foundations of several others. And the old Indians living on nearby islands would tell you the structure still standing was the Harem Shack.

They had other stories to tell—amusing tales of a mysterious Holy Man with uncut hair and a long beard the color of flame, a Holy Man who once sunned himself on the High Island beach while a dozen or more attractive young girls clustered about him and waited on him like servants; grim tales of hearing the weird animal-like screams of insane men and women who were held captive on that island, who were sometimes abandoned and left to die with a winter coming on.

If you'd been old enough, in the 1920's, to read the Detroit and Chicago newspapers—without having the latest exposé torn from their pages to shield your innocence—you knew that the Indian stories were true. For High Island, in a surprisingly recent era, was both the summer home and the prison camp of a very strange man, a man who created and reigned over an actual monarchy, a system of slavery more absolute than anything known in the Middle Ages, remaining in power for nearly a quarter of a century. The Conservation Department's announcement made a lot of people remember King

Ben—King of the Israelite House of David, King of the Flying Rollers—originally Benjamin Franklin Purnell.

The Indian tales were, in fact, only one small part of the truth, of the incredible saga of Ben Purnell. For High Island was but an outpost of his domain. His stronghold was several hundred miles to the south at Benton Harbor, directly across the lake from Chicago. And here, it was not only rumored but charged and proven in open court, he kept his subjects living at the lowest level of poverty and working long hard hours, while he himself resided in luxury in a mansion called Diamond House and the thousand-dollar bills in his vaults piled up into millions. Here he picked the prettiest of his subjects' daughters and ordered them sent to his palace, adding them to a collection matching that of any Arabian chieftain. Here he threatened instant death and eternal damnation for any who doubted or questioned or disobeyed him in the slightest.

Still, you might well remember King Ben more vividly from an earlier time, when you were too young to know the meaning of words like heresiarch or debauchery or despotism, when a trip to Benton Harbor was something like a trip to Disneyland today. All of the streetcar conductors had long hair and beards, and the older ones looked like Santa Claus. Down by the lake there was a fabulous amusement park, where other bearded men ran the concessions and rides, the roller coaster and the miniature railroad. If you were lucky enough to be there on the right day, you could go to the ballpark and watch a team of still other bearded men play a visiting team. It was a fantastic sight—three-foot-long manes of hair flying out behind them as they ran bases or chased flies and grounders. And they always won, usually by lopsided scores. There might even be a street parade. A bearded brass band would play, the ball team would march proudly behind them and the monarch who ruled over this wonderland might put in an appearance himself.

He never wore a crown, not in public anyway, but otherwise he lived up to all your expectations. Every stitch of his clothing was pure white. Beneath his fine white hat a great mass of coppered-colored curls fell down to drape over his shoulders, and his beard nearly hid his white tie. A massive gold locket hung from his neck, and if his white coat was unbuttoned, a heavy gold watch chain could be seen slung across his white vest. From a distance he looked something like the classic paintings of some ancient prophet. But if you could get close, you realized that there was something very strange about his eyes.

No matter how serious or stern he kept the rest of his face, they always seemed to be smiling—just as though, deep inside, he was constantly laughing at the whole world and everything in it.

Nothing in this account of the House of David under the rule of Mike Mills or Ben Purnell bears any known relation to the House of David as reorganized after Purnell's death and the unsuccessful attempt to resurrect him. In fact, the Supreme Court of Michigan ruled in 1929 that, although Ben Purnell's guilt had been incontrovertibly proven, the colony could very probably exist without him and not constitute in any way a menace to public morals. Furthermore, neither the State of Michigan nor the City of Benton Harbor have had cause to regret this decision.

Acknowledgments

THIS NARRATIVE is indebted to the Detroit *Free Press;* to the Detroit *News;* to the Benton Harbor *News-Palladium;* to the Burton Historical Collection of the Detroit Public Library; to Central Records Division, County Building, Ann Arbor, Michigan; to historian Milo M. Quaife for the chapter "The King of Benton Harbor," in his text *Lake Michigan;* to travel-writer Webb Waldron for the chapter "The House of David," in his book *We Visit the Great Lakes;* and to various other newspaper, magazine, text and personal sources no less helpful but too numerous for listing here. Although the married names of the former harem girls who returned to testify against King Ben Purnell were widely publicized both in the sensational exposés of 1923 and in the detailed coverage of the 1927 trial no useful purpose would be served by repeating them herein and only maiden names have been used whenever possible.

One

ONE DAY about seventy-seven years ago, a redheaded young hillbilly hobo, short on money but long on both charm and craftiness, made up his mind that there simply had to be an easier way of getting a bite to eat and a night's shelter than chopping wood for it. He was bumming his way across the flat farmlands of Ohio at the time, northward from his native Kentucky mountains, while his wife tagged along behind, as patient and uncomplaining as any Indian squaw. An abrupt inspiration came upon him.

Stopping at the next little town, he attended services at the local church, adding a fine lusty baritone to the singing but nothing to the collection plate, listened attentively to the sermon with an angelic smile, and slipped a hymn book under his shirt. Going next to the small local hotel, he started to rent a room for the night, then changed his mind after he'd inspected it, and a Gideon Bible had joined the hymnal. Finally, he used up the very last of his money on a white collar and a slightly used plain black coat. Then he took to the road again.

"Evening, Sister," he announced at the door of a farmhouse that night, while his wife stood beside him with her hands folded and a quiet simple smile on her thin drawn face. A plain drably dressed girl, she'd needed no disguise. "I'm the Reverend Benjamin Franklin Purnell. Are you happy in the Lord?"

Instead of receiving a back-door handout, Ben found himself being served the finest meal the humble farm family could offer, eating with their guest silver from their treasured little-used china. Instead of being sent to the hayloft, he was given the best room in the house. Just before he dropped off to sleep between fresh clean sheets under warm quilting, he happily promised himself that he'd never again chop another stick of firewood.

But even in his most fanciful dreams he couldn't possibly have guessed that this simple age-old trick would eventually enable him to amass a fortune estimated at ten million dollars, enjoy a harem of attractive young women rivaling even that of Solomon in all his glory, and establish and rule an actual kingdom in the very heart of Twentieth Century America.

Not too much is actually known of Ben Purnell's earliest years. He was born March 27, 1861, in a cabin in the hills near Maysville, Kentucky, of parents who were members of an obscure little religious sect known as Carmelites. A great deal of Biblical knowledge was whipped into him at an early age. Lengthy Biblical passages were so firmly committed to memory that he retained them his entire life. But otherwise he received very little formal schooling, just enough to read and write and handle simple figures. Gifted to the point of genius with an incredible instinctive grasp of human nature and human weakness, he never felt the lack of schooling.

"Horse manure is more useful than education," was his lifelong opinion. "If you put it on the ground and spread it, something grows and then you've got something."

Ben grew up good-looking, vain and lazy. There was something in his ever-laughing eyes that the girls liked, and from the beginning he liked the girls. He'd just turned sixteen when he decided to get married, picking a neighbor's daughter named Angelina Brown, moving in to live with her parents because he had no job and wasn't particularly interested in looking for one. But even then the notion that a fellow had to be satisfied with just one girl seemed ridiculous and unreasonable to him, and contrary to Nature. His marriage was a steady storm of quarreling over his attentions to other hillbilly girls.

"Where you going tonight?" his child bride would demand as he primped before a mirror, running a wet comb lovingly through his wavy red-gold hair.

"Visiting," he'd tell her.

"Visiting who?" Angelina would press him tearfully.

"Just visiting," he'd shrug.

Sometimes he'd be back the next morning. Just as often he'd be gone for weeks at a time. The hill people are patient people, and the Browns put up with this for more than two years. But when Angelina gave them a granddaughter to feed and clothe, they finally drew the line.

"Tell Ben to get himself a job and start bringing something into the home," they ordered her, "or else you tell him to get out!"

She gave him this ultimatum on the first evening of his next stay at the Brown cabin—hesitant and fearful, forcing firmness into her voice. She reminded him that he was a father, a family man now, and that he had yet to earn his first dollar, much less bring it home. He listened quietly and good-naturedly to her reasoning, then walked over to the mirror on the pine-boarded wall and began combing his hair.

"Where you going?" she asked, numbly and automatically.

"Visiting," he told her.

Forty-eight long years would pass before she saw him again. And then, white-haired and wrinkled, she would sit in a courtroom and add her brief story to the vast chronicle of evidence the Attorney General of the State of Michigan was assembling in his long hard fight to topple Ben Purnell from the throne of his kingdom.

Ben knocked about for several months and then met a girl named Mary Stollard, living just across the county line. Mary was 17, practically an old maid in the Kentucky hills, a thin quiet girl whom no one had ever called pretty. Ben Purnell was the first boy who'd payed much attention to her. From the beginning, she considered it nothing short of a Divine miracle that this handsome boy with the fetching way could be interested.

"You want to be my girl?" he asked her as they lay together on a hillside near the Stollard cabin, her head on his shoulder and her hair splashing over his chest, his fingers drifting lightly back and forth across her stomach.

"More than anything else in the world!" she told him fervently.

He gripped her waist, slid his hand up until his thumb stroked back and forth across her breast, then down again, along her slim thigh, flicking playfully at the hem of her skirt.

"You really want to be my girl?"

Her face was a little fearful now and her lips were quivering. But she nodded slowly.

He laughed then, a wet-throated self-certain chuckle, twisting sideways with one arm still beneath her, lifting his hand from her knee, cupping her cheek in it and watching her for a moment. Her eyes closed and her fingers dug into his shoulder. He kissed her once gently, then mouthed her lips demandingly until her teeth came apart, trembling. He laughed again as her breathing grew loud and rapid, and his kiss slid to her eyes, her ear, then to her throat. He could feel her heartbeat fluttering there beneath the smooth skin.

"Ben!" she gasped. "Ben!"

Nuzzling his forehead along her shoulder, his lips moved down to her breasts, caressing them gently, almost reverently, through the thin cotton cloth. When he kissed her again and began fumbling with the buttons below her throat, her body froze for a second and her hand moved up to push his away. But the gesture was weak and halfhearted. He caught her arm in his other hand and explored freely beneath her blouse, dropping his head back, letting it rise and fall slightly with her frenzied breathing as he cupped her breasts to his lips.

"My girl!" he assured her. And he laughed softly again.

She whimpered faintly, then something seemed to come alive within her. Her body began responding of its own accord to the practiced caresses of his stroking hands.

An indescribable feeling surged through him at that moment, something different than mere passion, a feeling of exultant omnipotence, of being gloriously and deliciously all-powerful. It was remotely like a feeling he'd known years earlier—hunting on the brushy slopes near his home, watching a bird or rabbit flushed from cover, snapping an old twin-hammered shotgun to his shoulder and knowing he wouldn't miss—but it was an infinitely deeper sensation, far more spine-tingling and compelling. He worked her clothing out of his way with sudden impatience, almost desperation.

She cried out once and shoved hard on his shoulders, her entire body flinching. But then, with her eyes still closed and each gasping breath a sob, she locked her arms about his neck and drummed her lips hungrily and eagerly against his.

Afterwards, as he was straightening his clothes and combing his hair, she lay still and looked up at him wonderingly.

"What's the matter, Ben?"

"Nothing." He shrugged. "There's just places I got to go, that's all."

"But Ben . . . I never did this before."

"I know it. You think I can't tell the difference?" He shrugged again. "So what? There's got to be a first time for everything."

"Why don't you stay here with us?" she asked eagerly. "Pa and Ma both like you. I know they do. They told me that any boy who knew more than half the Bible by heart was bound to be a good boy."

He considered the idea indifferently. "Maybe. I'll study on it some."

The Stollards, to Ben Purnell's way of thinking, were far more reasonable than the Browns had been. As long as their daughter was happy, they were perfectly willing to support this young man who'd moved in on them, willing to let him share their girl's bed with no nagging about getting out and looking for a job. And Ben kept Mary happy. In a way, he kept her parents happy, too.

"Say some of the Psalms for us again, Ben," they'd urge him as the four of them sat together before the fireplace in the evening. "I think that's the prettiest part of the whole Book."

Ben would let the phrases roll off his tongue melodically, while Mary smiled proudly.

"You got a real gift!" the Stollards would exclaim. "A real gift! You ought to make some use of it."

Even with a setup like this, Ben couldn't get out of the habit of going visiting, of rambling about through the hills in search of other girls. The first time Mary objected, he scolded her angrily and threatened to leave her.

"You want to hold onto a man, you let him act like a man," he warned her. "You expect me to eat just one kind of food, or wear just one set of clothes, or sit and look at just one bunch of hills my whole life? Well, this is no different! When this child feels like going visiting, he's going visiting!"

She never challenged his philosophy again. She merely counted herself blessed when he came back to her after each of his spells of restlessness.

Her family treated Ben Purnell like an honored guest for more than a year, not even asking his help with the chores. But a day finally came when Mr. Stollard took the boy aside for a man-to-man talk.

"Ben," he explained in an embarrassed voice, "the neighbors are starting to talk, and it's bothering Ma some. Don't you figure you and Mary had best marry up?"

Ben thought of Angelina for just a moment, then merely shrugged and nodded agreeably. Taking Mary across the state line to Aberdeen, Ohio, he religiously repeated his vows. Two more years passed before he made any attempt to divorce Angelina, and then he merely filed application, writing her that she was now a free woman, but never continuing the case and obtaining a decree.

(She soon found a new husband. Not until she was nearly 70 years old did she learn that her marriage, like Ben and Mary's, was bigamous.)

As pleasant and undemanding as life at the Stollard cabin was, Ben Purnell eventually grew bored with the scenery of his Kentucky hills and decided he'd set out to see the world. Mary went with him, of course. Her folks gave the young couple all the money they could afford and offered fervent prayers for their safety. For the hill people knew full well that sinfulness and evil were everywhere in the outside world.

To Ben's mind, though, the most disgusting evil he encountered was the fact that the outside world didn't seem to be nearly as susceptible to his charm as the hillbilly girls had been. The Ohio country people were hardened to the wiles of hobos. Each time he and Mary stopped at a farmhouse and he began to try to talk his way into a dinner invitation and a night's lodging, he was shown an ax and a woodpile or some other chore, while his wife was given work in the kitchen. Only after he'd strained and sweated for several hours was any food handed out. Back porches were their tables. Haylofts were their beds.

The sight of his wife slaving in other women's kitchens was something Ben Purnell could endure easily enough. And Mary herself never complained. But to have blisters forming on his previously smooth hands, to find wisps of straw in his fine head of hair each morning—this was unbearable.

"You got a real gift!" the Stollards had told him. "You ought to make some use of it."

It was then that he had that sudden revelation that was to shape his entire life.

Once Ben began posing as a traveling minister, a wayfaring evangelist, his technique improved steadily. The emotionalism of his native hills evidently supplied something missing and wanted in the quiet rural-Ohio church communities. In addition to supper and a sleeping place, he began trying his hand at preaching for spending money, holding brief street meetings in each new town.

"I used to be a sinner, just like you people!" His clear ringing voice would whip the curious and the bystanders on a main corner where any spectacle would bring a small gathering. "I used to live in a city just like this one, spending all my time in the hotels and saloons, drinking whiskey and smoking tobacco and loving-up to the painted women. But I saw the light, Brothers and Sisters. I felt the hand of the Lord heavy on my shoulder. I heard the call. So now I ask nothing more than the chance to bring His message to the people, the message in His Own Written Word."

One of the village loafers leaning against the nearest wall would make some snickering comment.

"There's always the ones that make fun of the Written Word when they hear it spoke." Ben would point out. "But I can tell you this, Brothers and Sisters—there's a time of reckoning coming. The small and the great'll stand before Him, the books'll be opened and every man judged according to his works."

He kept his sermons short at first, for he was still learning, still feeling his way along. Much of the time he merely repeated memorized Biblical passages and joined them together with phrases he'd heard the Carmelite preacher of his home church use. The result often bordered on gibberish, but Ben had a talent for remembering which words brought the best response and his preaching improved by a process of trial and error. A hymn or two followed, with Mary's thin anemic soprano adding a wavering overtone to his strong baritone. These were always the rhythmical old-time favorites and the crowd was always urged to join in. Immediately, Ben's hat would be passed, the small amount of change tossed into it pocketed, and the Purnells would be on their way, out on the road once more, searching out the most prosperous-looking farmhouse they could find before making their stop for the night.

Mary played her part in devout seriousness, for she didn't know she was playing a part. Ben told her he felt the Call and she believed him.

There were towns, of course, where self-appointed evangelists were unwelcome, where a deputy sheriff or constable escorted the Purnells right on through and suggested they keep moving, ignoring Ben's protests about the respect due a wearer of the cloth. There were frequent doors slammed in their faces. And more than once there were farmers who saw that this redheaded mountain boy's interest in their wives and daughters was something more than clerical. For even in the new role he was playing, Ben Purnell still experienced his old inherent difficulty in keeping his hands to himself whenever there was a pretty female about.

But there were also towns where a free-lancer's hat grew heavy with silver and homes where the Purnells were urged to stay on for days. There were even occcasional windfalls like lonesome widows or neglected farm wives whose men were off on hunting or stock-buying trips. Mary's presence was never any real drawback at such times.

If Ben woke her when he slipped quietly out of bed in the heavy hush of a country night, he'd meet her questions or protests with pious reminders about his duties as a minister. If she lay awake a while longer and listened, she'd invariably hear the low murmur of his voice, soft-toned and convincing, from another room. Sometimes he'd be back very quickly, cross and silent, and they'd leave at dawn without breakfast or even at once, in full darkness. Just as often, his faint whispered words would fade out in a prolonged silence or even the groaning of bedsprings, and she'd see him again only in the morning, feeling like an unwanted intruding chaperone as he continued to charm their hostess over coffee.

As his preaching became more and more skilled, there were any number of occasions when Ben might have settled down and become a respected member of a little rural community. The farm people of Ohio were deeply religious. This hillbilly boy had the gift of absolute sincerity in his voice, and women almost invariably liked him. But Benjamin Franklin Purnell found no attraction whatsoever in the threadbare life of a small-town lay minister.

Exactly what he was seeking, he didn't know himself. But he kept on looking, seldom walking the same road twice.

Two

THE FARM WIFE was short and round-faced, slightly plump. She seemed fidgety and flustered as Ben Purnell's voice purred silkily. Mary's face was expressionless as she stood beside her husband on the farmhouse porch. After seven years of marriage, she knew exactly what was coming and she was thoroughly conditioned to it.

"And so, Sister, we strive only to bring the light of the Written Word into the darkest corners of the countryside," Ben was saying. "We take no thought for the morrow, but merely trust in Christian goodness and charity to provide our simple needs—a little food, shelter for the night. The Lord has never failed us."

"You don't know how glad I am to see somebody." The woman was blushing slightly under the glow of the redheaded evangelist's eyes. "My man's off to show his team at the fair, off for the whole week-end, I guess. It gets mightly lonesome out this way."

"Before the warmth of Divine love, Sister, the chill of loneliness vanishes instantly," Ben assured her. "We will pray together tonight, you and I. And when you feel the Spirit growing and swelling within you, all of your doubts and fears will vanish and your loneliness will melt away."

A freckle-faced boy, perhaps twelve years old, stared suspiciously at Ben as he entered the parlor.

"What kinda preacher are you?" he demanded.

"A humble minister of God, Son." Ben smiled and reached out to pat his head. "Simply a preacher of His Written Word."

The boy ducked away. "You ain't the preacher from the reg'lar church!" he muttered stubbornly.

"You hush now!" his mother interceded. "You mind your manners!"

"No, no," Ben reproved her mildly. "That's a fine little lad you have. Except you be converted and become as little children, you shall not enter the kingdom. Blessed are the—" The cooking smells from the kitchen caught his nostrils abruptly, broadening his smile and interrupting his train of thought completely, snapping his head to the side like a hound striking a fresh trail. "Ah, yes!" he finished vaguely. "Blessed indeed!"

They sat down to a good meal and Benjamin Franklin Purnell's flowing talk was interrupted by his eating. He wolfed his food intently and purposefully, pausing only from time to time to flatter their hostess on her culinary skill. The woman was happily watching him eat, scarcely touching her own food and talking rapidly now, as though a plug had come loose inside her. Her talk was mostly complaint and self-pity—her isolation here in the middle of nowhere, how unfair it was for a girl who'd been raised in town and was used to better things, the never-ending drudgery of her life, her unappreciative and uncommunicative husband. Ben offered his sincere-voiced sympathy from time to time between mouthfuls. Mary's head began nodding. They'd walked a great disance that day, and this was an old familiar scene she'd sat through a hundred times. The young boy was strangely silent, but he kept right on glaring accusingly at the redheaded intruder.

They moved into the parlor after supper. Mary dozed off as Ben's voice droned on hypnotically, but their hostess hardly noticed her. The woman's attention was focused completely on this handsome young man who preached to her in tones that sounded almost as if he were making love, smoothly mixing Bible quotations with compliments that seemed even a little suggestive.

"The little lad seems to have disappeared," Ben mentioned once.

"Oh, he's off rambling somewhere," the farm wife said. "Off prowling the woods with that coon hound of his, most likely. He's just like his father."

"Should he be out on such a wet chilly night?" Ben Purnell seemed genuinely worried.

"Oh, a little rain and cold won't keep him home. Him or his father, either one. They're here to eat and to sleep and that's about it. How many evenings I've been left here by myself! Why . . ."

Several hours later, when the house was silent except for the steady sound of the wind outside, Mary heard Ben slipping out of bed beside her in the little-used first-floor room they'd been given.

"Where are you going?" she asked automatically.

"That poor woman is a troubled soul," he explained, softly and sadly. "It's my duty to minister to her needs, to give her what spiritual comfort I can."

Mary merely rolled over and was sleeping again before the sound of his footsteps reached the top of the stairs.

She woke up again, all at once. A hound was baying loudly outside. Voices came from the side yard, along with the rattle and creak of a harness.

There was a tremendous thump on the floor above her, then the frantic drumming of bare feet down the stairs. Ben Purnell burst back into the room.

"Grab your things!" he shouted in a whisper. "Come on!"

"What is it?" she asked sleepily. "What's the matter?"

"Never mind!" he hissed desperately. "Hurry up!"

As she fumbled clumsily and uncertainly in the darkness, he snatched up their clothing, crammed it into their cheap tin suitcase, then grabbed her wrist and started to pull her out of the room. The loud thud of footsteps came from the front porch, and he jerked her back, swinging their door closed, standing motionless just behind it.

"Don't make a sound!" he whispered in her ear. "Don't move!"

The front door slammed open. The hurried steps came directly down the hall, directly toward them. Ben Purnell's breathing cut out abruptly and his grip on Mary's wrist tightened painfully.

"I'll bet he ain't no real preacher atall!" The boy's

voice rang out, excited and happy. "I'll bet anything he ain't!"

"We'll see right quick!" A man's voice was gruff and snorting. "A fella from over Casstown was was tellin' me somethin' today. And if this's the same redheaded son-of-a . . ."

At the last moment, not a half-dozen steps away, the voices turned and went rapidly up the stairs.

"Now!" Ben's breath came out in a gasp. "Let's go!"

He swung their door open and yanked her down the hall with him, out across the front porch and through the mud of the yard. Still barefoot and in night clothes, they went down the road at a full run, the suitcase swinging from one of Ben's hands, his other still locked about Mary's wrist. The night was very dark—rain was still falling. Mary couldn't keep up. He dragged her along, sliding and stumbling.

"Wait a minute, Ben!" she begged. "Wait!"

"Hush!" He looked back down the road, then turned and yanked her into a dense thicket, the load of water in the branches splashing down on their already wet bodies, soaking and chilling them. They crouched there, motionless, as a team and wagon splashed loudly by, a dim hunched figure cursing at the horses and lashing at them with the reins.

When the wagon had gone on out of hearing, Ben pushed on through the brush to a small clearing, where they hurriedly dressed in darkness. They waited there silently until they heard the wagon clattering back toward the farmhouse, back to search in the other direction. Then they fumbled their way out through the thicket and on down the road. The rain was slackening now. The first light of dawn was just coming into the sky.

"He wouldn't have understood at all," Ben mentioned. "From what that poor soul had to say, he wasn't an understanding man."

"Ben," Mary complained hesitantly. "I can't do like this much longer."

"We do only what the Lord has willed we do!" he

reminded her. The cold impatience of his voice contrasted strongly with the warm sympathetic tone he'd used on their hostess the night before.

"But I'm going—" Held back for weeks now, she finally choked it out. "I'm going to have a baby."

He stood silent for a long time. In the early dimness, she couldn't see his face.

"It's all right, isn't it, Ben?" she begged fearfully. "Tell me it's all right!"

"We must never question what the Lord sends our way," he finally answered. His voice was dull and toneless.

They kept on traveling, working the little Ohio towns near the Indiana border now. But winter was coming on and Mary's time was growing steadily nearer. Ben had to face up to the future. He could abandon her, as he'd done Angelina. Or he could begin providing, at least for a time, a little more of a home than the one-night stops at farmhouses.

There is no reason for supposing that any degree of human affection entered into the choice he made, for there is simply no evidence that Ben Purnell, at any time throughout his entire life, ever felt affection for anybody but Ben Purnell. More likely, he merely realized that Mary had become a valuable asset, adding a degree of respectability to the role he'd assumed. Besides, Ben was a man who didn't care to run the risk of sleeping alone very many nights, and wives as broad-minded as this one were hard to come by. At any rate, he finally gritted his teeth and went across the state line into Richmond to look for a job.

Twenty-six years old at the time, this was a completely new experience for him. He turned on all of his charm and outdid himself with sincerity in an attempt to find employment that didn't involve work, but nowhere were women doing the hiring. He ended up as a common laborer in a broom factory.

He found a cheap furnished flat and eventually paid a midwife to see Mary through her time. But after the baby was born, a girl they named Hettie, Ben Purnell decided to stay on in Richmond. His restlessness was momentarily forgotten. He'd discovered a new interest now.

He'd become extremely fascinated by the teachings and history of a strange cult of religious fanatics who called themselves Israelites.

Back in the year 1792, a poverty-stricken English charwoman named Johanna Southcott had suddenly gone into a trance, then awakened from it insisting that she was a prophet, the first of Seven Divine Messengers who would be sent down from heaven in a last-ditch attempt to save the world from Satan. The Lord had chosen her to bring together an "In-gathering" of 144,000, she'd announced. When the final Seventh Angelic Messenger arrived—she'd decided from an imaginative interpretation of the Book of Revelations—all who believed in him would enjoy the Millennium, the thousand years of peace and plenty, while the rest of humanity would perish. Through the next 20 years, she'd accumulated a vast fortune and about 100,000 followers —short of the goal the Lord had set but still a sizable congregation. She'd also turned out dozens of religious pamphlets which became the Sacred Writings of the sect.

Finally, in the year 1814, Johanna had announced that she would bring forth the Second Messenger by immaculate conception. Since she was 65 years old at the time, this had been a joke to all but her devoted followers. Then suddenly her stomach had started to swell. Some doctors who'd examined her had insisted these symptoms were strictly psychological; others had asserted she was really pregnant; and this medical debate had been carried on vigorously in the pages of the London *Times*. The Israelites had joyfully prepared for the arrival of the Messiah they called Shiloh, even having a solid gold cradle built. But the old woman's stomach had collapsed abruptly and the doctors attending her had pronounced her dead. She'd died trying.

Quite naturally, in the years that followed, others had

made use of the same path to power and riches, proclaiming themselves Divine Messengers and keeping the Israelite cult alive, announcing new revelations, broadening Johanna Southcott's original concept with new liturgy. The Second Messenger had been Richard Brothers; the third, George Turner; the fourth, William Shaw. The Israelites had been split repeatedly by rival Messengers denouncing and branding each other as heresiarchs, and the factionalism and in-fighting had caused the loss of a good share of the original converts. But not until the 1850's, when a man named John Wroe had proclaimed himself the Fifth Angelic Messenger, had any amount of public scandal come to the cult.

John Wroe's revelations had told him that shaves and haircuts were to be outlawed from that time on. They'd also told him that all young girls were to be sent to him for a rite he'd described as "cleansing of the blood" or "female circumcision", which meant simply that he demanded first choice of the virgins of the sect. Wroe's Biblical justification for this had been that if young boys were unclean in the eyes of God without circumcision, young girls were also unclean without a similar severing of tissue and letting of blood.

Under the leadership of a man named John Ward, a large proportion of the Israelites had refused to accept these innovations and had turned apostate, calling themselves Southcottites and following only Johanna's original teachings. But John Wroe had tightened his hold on those who remained, the faction known as Wroeites, and had put his perverted practises into effect, even winning new converts through endless missionary tours. Modern experts believe he was hopelessly insane; if a madman, he was a shrewd and convincing madman. But as a result of his leadership, the long-haired bearded Wroeites had been driven out of England by public indignation and mob violence, migrating in large numbers to Australia, Canada and the North-Central United States.

Living in Australia, John Wroe had received a revelation that the Millennium would begin in 1863. When he'd abruptly passed away early in February of that year his loyal followers had been overjoyed, taking this as a sign that he was merely repeating the pattern of the last days of Christ, that he would soon be returning from the dead to lead them into their thousand years of reward. But the "Beardies", as the Australians called them, had waited in vain, both for the resurrection and the Millennium.

Some years later, when the Israelites had tired of waiting for Wroe to come back, an Australian sailor named James White had proclaimed himself the Sixth Messenger, changing his name to James Jezreel. ("Then shall the children of Judah and the children of Israel be gathered together . . . for great shall be the day of Jezreel." Hosea 1:11.) He'd ruled the cult until early in the 1880's. His main contribution to Israelite history had been the writing and publishing of a book entitled *The Flying Roll*, a book specifically designed to be circulated among outsiders in the hope of making converts out of them. The book had been pretty much of a failure. Few converts had been won. In fact, the sect had steadily lost members until less than a thousand people, scattered across three continents, still clung to the old faith. But *The Flying Roll* had brought one noticeable result. From the time of its appearance, the bearded cultists who'd attempted to peddle it from door to door had been popularly known as Flying Rollers.

(Not to be confused with "Holy Rollers" or Pentecostals. Nor should this strange cult be regarded as any offshoot of Judaism. Because they called themselves Israelites, the cultists were often referred to by outsiders of the regions where they settled as "a bunch of Jews." They were not Jewish. With a very few exceptions, their background lay in the smaller, more-emotional sects of Christian Protestantism.)

By the late 1880's, the Flying Rollers were breathlessly awaiting the coming of the final Seventh Angelic Messenger, the Messiah who would lead them into the

Millennium, their thousand years of reward during which they would have the pleasure of watching the rest of humanity perish.

The century-long record of scandal delighted Ben Purnell. Here was a religion that seemed to be tailored to order for him. Eagerly, he read and re-read *The Flying Roll* and all the other sacred pamphlets and writings the handful of long-haired bearded cultists living Richmond could obtain for him.

"This is the True Faith," he explained to Mary. "Everything else is nothing more than blasphemy in the eyes of the Lord. This is the path we must follow."

She didn't question him.

Ben's real plan, of course, was to proclaim himself the Seventh Messenger, to create and enjoy the same kind of personal heaven John Wroe had known. But first he had to win the confidence and trust of the cultists, to make himself well enough known so that when the time came for his attempt to take over, his claim would sound reasonable and be accepted.

Ben gave up his career as a broom-maker and worked feverishly, devoting every minute of his time to this new scheme, knocking on half the doors in town with copies of *The Flying Roll* under his arm, letting his red-gold hair grow longer and the beginnings of a beard come onto his face, preaching constantly to win new converts.

"The Millennium is close at hand!" he shouted on every street corner in Richmond. "Whosoever is not found written in the Book of Life shall be cast into the lake of fire! Are you ready, Brothers and Sisters? Is your name there in the Roll to be called by the Master?"

Before long Ben Purnell was the accepted leader of the local group of cultists. Gradually he began making a name for himself among the Flying Rollers of other Indiana and Ohio towns. But just as he was almost ready for the final gamble, word arrived that someone had beaten him to it. A man named Michael Keyfor Mills, well known among the Israelites and now calling himself Prince Michael ("And at that time shall Michael stand up, the great prince . . . and at that time the people shall be delivered, every one that shall be found written in the book." Daniel 12:1.), had just received a revelation telling him he was the Seventh Angelic Messenger and was estiblishing the Seventh Kingdom in Detroit, Michigan, calling it the New and Latter House of Israel.

Secretly furious and sick with disappointment, Ben toyed for a time with the idea of having a revelation of his own, denouncing Prince Mike as an imposter and heresiarch, calling on the cultist to desert Mills and come to Richmond. But he finally put aside the notion. Still, he couldn't quit now. He couldn't throw away several years of work. In January of 1892 he decided to move to Detroit to join the new colony.

"We must hurry to join the In-gathering," he informed Mary. "The Millennium could come any day now."

Again she didn't question him. She never questioned him.

The moment Benjamin Franklin Purnell met Michael Keyfor Mills he realized that the new Divine Messenger was no religious fanatic, but merely another opportunist like himself. Nearly a hundred of the bearded Israelites had rushed to find quarters in the district that surrounded Mills' home, which he now called God-House, at #37 Hamlin Avenue on the North Side of Detroit. And already their Messenger was playing them for all he could get, bleeding the "Little People" of the sect unmercifully.

To prove themselves fit to enjoy the Millennium, all who joined the New and Latter House of Israel were expected to give up earthly wealth—give it up to Mike Mills, of course. Since there was no room for idle hands in the Seventh Kingdom, all of the faithful, men and women alike, were required to work at full-time jobs and to spend every spare moment peddling *The Flying Roll* from door to door in hopes of bringing in more converts, as well as the profits from the book. To keep his followers free from temptation, the Prince relieved them of all their earnings, then generously returned just enough for a bare subsistence.

The redheaded young man from the Kentucky hills was deeply impressed by all this. But he was even more impressed by the fact that Mike Mills had already managed to resurrect the old Wroeite practice of blood-cleansing, of female circumcision—demanding not only the wages but also the daughters of his followers.

Although his wife was still living at God-House, the Prince had brought in seven or eight other women to join her there. He called them "pieces of the God-Head." They were supposed to number 10, eventually, and each piece was supposedly there to symbolize and exemplify some desirable virtue to the Little People of the New and Latter House of Israel. In age they ranged from 49-year-old Eliza Court, a hatchet-faced woman with graying hair who personified Spiritual Affinity, to a strikingly beautiful 15-year-old girl named Bernice Bickle, who personified Obedience.

The Prince gave a warm welcome to the new arrivals from Richmond. Mike Mills had already heard of Ben Purnell and his energetic laboring in behalf of the Israel-ites. Noticing his impressive appearance and his convincing tone of voice immediately, Mills realized full well that this redheaded hillbilly could be an extremely valuable lieutenant for him in the scheme of things he was creating. Besides, he took a liking to the younger man. Only a few days passed before a new trance descended upon Prince Mike, with the revelation that Ben Purnell had been Divinely chosen a Pillar of Israel, a rank second only to that of the Messenger himself.

A Pillar was exempt from the requirement of holding an outside job, and in addition enjoyed a higher standard of living than his fellow cultists, the Little People. Both his food and his quarters were better. A Pillar's duties consisted entirely of enforcing the Messenger's edicts and making missionary tours. In return for this privileged status, the Prince expected gratitude, loyalty and unqualified support in all things. Purnell was definitely one man Millis wanted in his own corner.

But what Prince Michael Mills somehow failed to realize was that Benjamin Franklin Purnell, from his very first days at Detroit, was constantly scheming and plotting to overthrow and replace him.

Three

AT THE TIME when Ben, Mary and little Hettie Purnell first arrived at the New and Latter House of Israel, Mike Mills was having harem trouble. Lovely young Bernice Bickle wanted no part of this lecherous long-haired man more than twice her age, Angelic Messenger or not. Obedience was stubbornly refusing to obey her Prince.

Mills had known William and Elizabeth Bickle, who lived across the river in Toronto, for some time. They were Israelites in good standing, devoted followers of his. But not until the autumn before had he particularly noticed their daughter, now budding out in a way that belied her age. Playing the piano and singing hymns at a revival meeting, she'd made a deep and lasting impression on him.

Bernice was a blue-eyed pouting-lipped young lady, round-faced, almost doll-like with her light-brown hair in the ringlets that were fashionable at the time. Only a few faint freckles remained on her cheeks as reminders that she was scarcely more than a child. Her parents had been investing for many years in her piano and voice lessons; her playing was mature and skilled, her singing warm and husky.

But it was the fresh near-plumpness of her young body that caught and held the eye of the bearded prophet—breasts that strained enticingly, playing fantastic tricks with her blouse on each of the quick breaths she drew between hymn stanzas; full-fleshed, rounded hips that even the drab loose-cut skirts considered proper for Israelite daughters could not hide. Prince Michael had returned to his God-House in Detroit, slumped immediately into a trance, then come awake to announce a new revelation—the Almighty had ordered that the 15-year-old Bickle girl become the Tenth Piece in the God-Head.

Writing to the Bickles to give them the news, he'd sent $10, suggesting they change it into 10 Canadian gold pieces as a present for Bernice. He'd cited the parable of the talents, also insisting that the gold pieces would represent the 10 pieces in the God-Head, but the money had actually been a bribe. The girl's parents had been highly flattered, and they'd moved immediately into the Detroit colony.

Honoring her mother and father, as her Bible told her to do, Bernice had obeyed their order that she go to live in Mills' God-House on Hamlin Avenue while they rented quarters elsewhere. But nothing in the Scripture had prepared her for the eager-eyed, eager-handed, long-bearded man who'd greeted her.

"My sweet little Bernice!" He gripped her shoulders tightly. "Welcome to God-House, my dear. Come to me!"

Her body stiffened. She closed her eyes and bit her lower lip as that strange-eyed face, framed completely by long hair, moved down on her, as he pulled her against him and kissed her gently on the forehead, his beard bristling against her nose and mouth. But when his hand left her shoulders and moved on down her sides with his thumbs and fingers digging in hungrily, she shoved hard against him and then backed away crying.

"I want to go home! I don't want to stay here!"

"Bernice!" Shaking his head slowly, he smiled. "You're tired and upset, child. You were called by the Lord to come and place yourself in Obedience to Michael, His son. It has been revealed that you represent the Tenth Piece in the God-Head. All Israel envies you. Of course, you want to stay!"

She glanced fearfully at him, then looked away again.
"I don't like it when you grab me like that," she
pouted.

Patient and generous, Prince Mike gave her two
whole days to become acclimatized. He sent her to
sleep with his wife and an older harem-member the first
night. On the second, he had her share a room with another young newcomer, a girl who didn't seem quite as
rebellious. He visited the two of them that evening,
giving them a box of candy, sitting on the side of the
bed and talking to them for nearly an hour, then saying
good night. On the third evening, he ordered Bernice
sent to his room, waiting until he was sure she was in
bed before entering.

"Dear Bernice" He took her hand and patted it.
"When I first heard you playing the piano so beautifully, I dreamt that some day you would play for us
here at God-House."

She stared at him in suspicious silence.

"When the In-gathering of Israel is completed, my
dear, you'll play before the vast throng of one hundred
and forty-four thousand. I promise you that."

Quickly and matter-of-factly, he shed his clothes and
slipped into bed beside her.

"What are you doing?" she demanded.

Smiling kindly, he explained that this was something
necessary to her salvation, an essential part of preparing
her for an important role in the only society that would
exist once the Millennium came. In great detail he
described the beauties and wonders of the kingdom that
awaited those who were faithful and loyal and obedi-
ent to the Seventh Divine Messenger. It was not her
place to try to understand all the intricacies of the various ways her fitness for the Millennium might be tested,
he pointed out, only to have faith in the word of God
as it came down through his servants, the prophets.

"You are to symbolize Obedience to all Israel," he told
her. "Are you willing to obey me, Bernice?" He let his
fingers trail lightly along her leg.

"No!" she decided. "Not like that!"

"Dear Bernice!" He shook his head, smiling. "You must obey me in everything."

He slipped his arm around her, pulled her against him and rubbed her back.

"No!" She stiffened at his touch.

Still smiling, he explained to her that the Divine fire had burned all evil out of his body, leaving him completely pure, and that all he wanted to do was to sow the seeds of the same purity in her—that if this was not done, Satan would sow evil there. Whispering his arguments close to her ear, he let his lips move up into her hair, then back down across the warm curve of her neck. He began kissing her breasts reverently through the flimsy material of her nightgown, then slid his hand hungrily into the baby-soft coolness.

Her body tightened with anger and she tried to push him away. He held her there, struggling and breathing hard, for a long moment, staring wet-eyed at the way her fast-pulsing gasps played tricks with the cloth of her gown. But when she began screaming, he gave up for the time being.

"Choose what you want," he warned her grimly, "life or death. The Lord will have a willing people and none other." He then turned his attention to cleansing the blood of Bernice's less-stubborn roommate of the night before.

Several weeks passed before he made another attempt on the rebellious new harem member. During this time Eliza Court, the senior piece in the God-Head, worked on her steadily. With sharp hissing words and an occasional stinging slap, the older woman reminded Bernice that being here was a great honor and privilege and urged her to do as she was told.

"Don't you realize Prince Michael's is different from other men, you little fool?" she snapped. "Can't you understand that everything he does is right and good?"

"No!" the teen-age girl pouted.

Eliza failed, and once again Prince Mike ordered Bernice sent to his room. This time he armed himself with a Bible, a copy of *The Flying Roll* and a number of the old Wroeite sermons. For several hours he read and interpreted various passages for her. But once again, when he slid into bed beside her, she pulled away.

"You're a little tease, aren't you?" His preaching voice gave way to a soft chuckle.

"No, I'm not"

Still laughing, he reached over and lifted her nightgown. She jerked it back down immediately. He jumped up in exasperation.

"The Lord is extremely angry!" he warned her. "For three full weeks I've allowed a person of unclean blood to occupy an exalted position in his abode, and a mockery has been made of the virtue of Obedience. Unless your blood is cleansed very quickly, you'll be in your grave."

Bernice lay awake most of the night, sobbing softly. Raised by fanatic parents, she was deeply religious. Fear of death and eternal punishment racked her young body—visions of fire and brimstone tortured her mind.

Prince Mike gave her more than another month to become adjusted to the situation, to realize that all the other girls were accepting his unique form of ministering. During this time, he took all the pieces of the God-Head with him on a missionary tour to England, enjoying a luxurious ocean voyage while the cultists went on slaving to support him. But upon his return to Detrort, he found himself unable to think of anything else but this infuriating, maddening, still-unclaimed little beauty. And he'd sent Eliza Court to bring Bernice once again to his room.

"With whom have you been sleeping, child?" he asked in the tone of voice a schoolmaster might use to scold a pupil.

"With Mrs. Mills," she choked, afraid of him.

He nodded grimly. "I thought so. Do you know that Mrs. Mills is evil and rebellious, Bernice? Do you know that I've had to put handcuffs on her and lock her in the closet more than once? Do you want me to have to do that with you?"

"No."

"All right, then. You're to sleep with Sister Eliza and myself in the hope that our purity can combat the evil you've contracted from Mrs. Mills."

The three of them lay together for some time that night, while Prince Mike and Sister Eliza lectured the girl on the necessity of having the seeds of purity planted in her blood. Eventually, the long-haired Prince tapped his senior harem-member on the shoulder, and she slipped out of bed and left the room.

"Now, Bernice," Mike Mills announced grimly. "I must have Obedience!"

Her entire body was shaking, tightening and wrinkling her nightgown enticingly. He caught both her wrists, twisted them behind her back and held them there with one hand, while the other caressed her legs, then explored beneath her gown, moving up along the fullness of her young thighs, across the slight roundness of her stomach, on to her heaving breasts. Her head was moving steadily from side to side. Her crying, her attempts to twist away, the steady shuddering of her shoulders, the trembling of her teeth when he kissed her—all this served only to heighten his excitement and eagerness.

"Stop it!" she begged. "Please stop it!"

"Hold still, goddamn it!" he snarled in a shouted whisper.

With the full weight of his chest and shoulders pinning her tightly, with her arms locked numbly beneath her, she tried to jerk her knees up to block him, but he forced them back down. His mouth was searching steadily for the lips that twisted away from his kisses, his beard dragging over her throat, his long hair hanging down on all sides of her head. His free hand tugged her nightgown on up, fumbled for a moment beneath him, then joined his other behind her. He let her arms go free as his own clenched her tightly against him, but she could only beat her fists weakly and futilely against his sides.

"Please don't!" she sobbed. "You're hurting me!"

Obedience was finally obtained. The God-Head was complete. Israel was secure.

As Benjamin Purnell looked over the Prince's domain in open admiration and hidden envy, he immediately spotted the one serious flaw in the very foundations of the New and Latter House of Israel, the single vulnerable point at which a shrewd and skilled attack might very well topple the entire structure. The legal Mrs. Mills, now living in God-House and treated like just another piece of the God-Head by the Prince, was a jealous and vengeful woman—as unreasonable, Ben Purnell decide, as his own first wife Angelina had been.

Ben could see nothing in Sister Mills that remotely resembled attractiveness, but business was business and first things had to come first. He combed out his colorful hair, groomed his new beard and went to work. While Prince Mike was amusing himself with teen-agers. Ben Purnell turned every ounce of his charm loose on the Prince's wife.

At first he merely listened sympathetically to her complaints about the way her husband was mistreating her, tenderly comforting her loneliness. But gradually, as the weeks went by and their relationship became very close, he began subtly feeding her anger and encouraging her growing dissatisfaction.

"Don't you sometimes think it's strange?" He'd be puzzled, sincerely puzzled, because at all times and above all else, Benjamin Purnell was convincingly sincere. "It was a woman who organized the Israelites in the first place, but all of the Messengers ever since have been men. Why, except for Sister Eliza, not one of the Pillars here is a woman!"

"I've had my doubts about Michael for a long, long time," she'd confide in a whisper as they huddled together in some secluded corner. "These people here think he's an angel from Heaven, but there's some things I could tell you, believe me! He never even heard of the Israelites until four years ago. And before that . . . well, all I can say is that he just wasn't the kind of man the Good Lord would pick to do His work, not by a long sight!"

"I wouldn't think of questioning the Prince!" Ben

would be shocked at the very thought. "But there's one other thing I can't help wondering about. I've read just about everything Johanna Southcott ever wrote. I can't find a thing about this God-Head business there."

"Those girls just might not be around here too much longer," Mrs. Mills would hint mysteriously.

Naturally enough, Ben was playing both sides of the street. Having worked his way into Mike Mills' confidence, he egged him on in every conceivable way to infuriate his wife still further.

"Prince Michael, there's something I think I ought to tell you." He'd approach the Divine Messenger with the pained solemn look of a man performing an unpleasant but necessary duty.

"Certainly, Brother Benjamin," The Prince would put him at ease. "What is it?"

"Well . . . a lot of the women are complaining. About Sister Mills. They say she's getting all kinds of extra privileges. They say she doesn't work and never goes out to sell the Sacred Writings or anything, and yet she lives better than any of the rest of them. The way they see it, just the fact that you were married to her before the soul of the Angelic Messenger entered into you doesn't entitle her to all that. I just thought I ought to tell you."

Prince Mike would nod slowly. "I'm pleased you did, Brother Benjamin. I'll take this problem under careful consideration."

From the beginning, Ben Purnell was confident that this line of attack would eventually unseat the Prince. But he was pleasantly surprised when it took only a few months. The explosion came that spring, even more violent than he'd intended. He lit the final fuse by approaching Mike Mills with a new suggestion.

"Some of the men are feeling envy, Prince Michael. And envy's an evil thing."

"What kind of envy, Brother Benjamin?"

"Envy because of the girls in the God-Head," Ben told him.

The Seventh Angelic Messenger blew his top. "They

have no right! That is naked heresy. None of them has any right to question me. Their duty is to obey God's orders as they come down through me in revelation!"

"I know. I know." Ben soothed him. "It's just that they're only human and human flesh is weak."

"I have no patience with such weakness."

"I'd never have mentioned it, except that I had an idea how to destroy this envy."

"I see no need to pamper heresy!" The Prince had been firm, warily guarding against any suggestion that he share his harem.

"No, of course not," Ben agreed. "But suppose you set up a system—the Almighty willing, of course—for the Little People to swap wives once in a while? I've been reading in John Wroe's writings that a system like that will be used in the final kingdom to wipe out envy, to prevent one man from coveting another's wife. Maybe it should be started now."

Prince Mike considered this carefully, then told his chief Pillar that he'd have to wait for word from Higher Up. But evidently the idea appealed to Mills. Just a few days later there was a new trance, a new revelation and a new edict for the Israelites. From now on the wives of the colony would be rotated among the men on a fair and impartial basis.

For Sister Mills, this was the last straw. A chummy secret friendship with a good-looking young man was one thing. Being passed from crackpot to crackpot in this weird community was something else entirely. When the Prince told her she would have to obey his edicts the same as any other Israelite woman, she set the halls of God-House ringing with loud language that didn't resemble Bible quotations in the slightest, slammed out the front door and marched directly to the office of the first lawyer she could find. She then initiated suit for divorce, naming Eliza Court as co-respondent, naming the Prince's other mistresses in her charges and talking freely about what had gone on in the New and Latter House of Israel to anyone who cared to listen, reporters included.

Once the details of bedroom life at God-House came out in the Detroit newspapers, strong public feeling was aroused. On March 30 a large mob of North Side citizens marched up Hamlin Avenue, massed tightly in front of Mills' home and began smashing the windows.

"Out with the Long-Hairs! Burn 'em out! Burn 'em out!" they chanted murderously, very much like a cheering section at a football game. "Out with the Long-Hairs! Burn 'em out! Burn 'em out!"

The police arrived in time to disperse the crowd, but Mike Mills saw what was in the wind. With elaborate cryptic oaths, he swore each of his harem-girls to secrecy, then called a meeting of the Pillars of Israel.

"I have been Divinely commissioned to preach the Israelite gospel over the entire world, not merely here in this little corner," he announced.

Ben Purnell and the other noticed that he was extremely nervous, that his hands were shaking. Very suddenly, the bearded Prince began singing a well-known missionary hymn.

"In the deserts let me labor, on the mountains let
* me tell,*
*   How he died, the blessed Savior, to redeem a world*
*   from hell!*
*   Let me hasten . . . far in heathen lands to dwell."*

Just as abruptly, the long-haired prophet's singing stopped. "Do any of you know how far it is to New Zealand?" he demanded.

Ben and the other Pillars scratched their heads and exchanged puzzled glances.

"Or possibly Australia?" the Seventh Messenger asked weakly.

It was too late for running, though. A newly formed committee of angry North Side citizens had convinced Mrs. Mills she should sign a criminal complaint charging both Mike and Eliza with lascivious co-habitation; and on April 11 the police raided God-House, arresting the Prince and his Spiritual Affinity, taking the other harem-members into protective custody. Dragged down Hamlin Avenue kicking and shouting, Prince Michael called down every curse imaginable upon the heads of the officers.

"You will all die horribly!" he shrieked. "All who are involved in this outrage will die of a horrible disease!"

He was hauled into Recorder's Court and brought before the Honorable Fitzwilliam H. Chambers for a preliminary hearing.

"How do you plead to this charge?" the judge asked.

"I refuse to plead before an earthly court," Mills told him. "Only God can judge me."

"Are you represented by counsel?"

"I have no need of earthly counsel. God is my counsel and God will protect me."

In spite of the way he sounded, Mike Mills was no fool. When the legal firm of Atkinson, Carpenter, Brooks & Haigh, headed by the famous Colonel John Atkinson, one of the greatest criminal lawyers in the country, volunteered to defend him free of charge, the Prince swallowed his contempt for earthly counsel and received the new revelation that God was willing to share his defense with a mere lawyer. Mrs. Mills suffered a nervous breakdown, dropped her charges and fled into Canada. But by that time several of the harem girls had given statements and new charges were ready. Colonel Atkinson filed a plea of not guilty for the Prince on May 4.

Immediately after the arrest, the police and public officials had been pestered constantly by angry Flying Rollers who'd protested this blasphemy, this insult to their leaders and degradation of their faith. And no one had been lounder and more eloquent in condemning this outrage than Ben Purnell, who'd worked tirelessly for months to bring it about.

But the authorities had a far more serious problem on their hands than the indignation of the Israelites. As the people of Detroit began waking up to what had gone on in their midst, as the pathetic stories told by Bernice Bickle and the other girls were played for all they were worth in boosting newspaper circulation, public fury became murderous. At a gigantic mass meet held at

Brown's Hall, lynching was openly advocated, even though police were present. The press was screaming for blood.

AFTER THE LONG-HAIRS! THEY MUST GET OUT OF THE NORTH SIDE OF DETROIT! one editorial was headed.

FLYING ROLLER COLONY—NORTH SIDE CITIZENS WANT IT WIPED OUT! another stated.

The home of Israelite William Brown, on Lyman Place, was mobbed in mid-May. Every window was broken and the entire front of the house was smashed in.

A short time later, Israelite Thomas Dooley, walking with his wife down Hamlin Avenue, was captured by another mob. Mrs. Dooley was shoved roughly aside and her husband was publicly horsewhipped.

Not long afterwards, Prince Michael set out to walk to the offices of Atkinson, Carpenter, Brooks & Haigh for a strategy conference. Ben Purnell and another trusted Pillar named Ed Durand went with him. A few outsiders had followed Durand from his home at 706 Wabash, jeering him constantly. As the three long-haired, bearded men hurried on their way, the crowd grew steadily larger, collecting new hecklers at every corner. Obscenities were shouted. Violence seemed certain to come. But Mills and Purnell and Durand finally ducked safely into the office building.

After a long conference with Colonel Atkinson, Prince Mike emerged smiling. The colonel had been unable to defeat a prosecution move to have his bail increased from $1000 to $3000, and the money would have to be raised somehow. In some way, a full report of that meeting at which he'd asked about New Zealand and Australia had gotten into the hands of the police. (Ben Purnell was sincerely indignant. Was there a traitor among the Pillars?) Even so, Mills seemed happy, genuinely confident, more sure of himself than he'd been at any time since his arrest. The colonel had ordered him to tell absolutely no one what they'd talked about, but he'd say this much—the Lord would be providing a few tricks in behalf of his faithful servant. Look for a couple of big surprises, he hinted.

The smile vanished from the Prince's face when they left the building. The crowd outside had grown steadily. Several thousand people were massed there now, and their angry muttering was becoming a strange growling roar, the unearthly sound of a crowd becoming a mob. The three Israelite men were trapped against a wall.

Prince Mike waved his arms and tried to talk to them. "Let he who is without sin cast the first stone!" he shouted.

But the first stone had already been cast, along with heavy sticks, pieces of coal, and apples and potatoes from an overturned vender's cart. Missiles snarled through the air in a steady shower. Ben Purnell and Ed Durand buried their faces in their arms and huddled against the brick wall, but the Prince went on attempting to preach to the mob. Struck several times in the face, he was bleeding badly. A half-dozen men rushed in and began clubbing him.

Suddenly, the shrill sounds of police whistles split the air. Skillfully and efficiently, at considerable risk to their own necks, the officers fought their way through to drive off the attackers with swinging night-sticks, forming a tight ring around the three bearded men and protecting them while other members of the Detroit police began the long tricky task of breaking up the mob. (This was the same Detroit police department Prince Mike's attorney would later attack viciously, accusing the officers of everything from joining a conspiracy against the Prince to taking indecent liberties with the harem girls who were being held in protective custody at the Woodbridge police station.)

The long-haired prophet was safe for the moment, but the situation was growing steadily more dangerous. New lynch mobs kept forming and were broken up, only to form again, immediately. The Israelites were stoned and beaten whenever they were seen on the street. There seemed little chance of the Prince ever

getting to trial alive, and finally the state troopers
smuggled him off to Ann Arbor, with a change of
venue being granted on June 6.

In that sleepy little college town, the trial of the
bearded prophet was, of course, a sensational one. On
its opening day, June 14, class attendance at the Uni-
versity of Michigan hit an all-time low, as the students
rushed to the county courthouse for a glimpse into a
brand of theology seldom discussed in texts. Every seat
in the courtroom was taken. The hall outside was tightly
jammed. Even the courthouse lawn was crowded.

In an attempt to lessen the embarrassment of the girls
who had to testify, no male spectators were allowed in
the first two rows of benches on the side that faced the
witness stand. This section was tied off with a white
ribbon and reserved for an organized group of older
woman from various reputable churches who were
there specifically to sympathize with and encourage the
former harem girls.

In the row on the other side reserved for defense witnesses, a number of Israelite Pillars and even a few of
the Little People waited to testify for their Prince, to
describe his immaculate character and his purity of conduct. Benjamin Franklin Purnell sat among them, and
like the rest, his face was frozen into a bitter grimace
of self-righteousness, of distaste for this absurd indignity.

But unlike the rest, his eyes were smiling. His eyes
were practically laughing out loud.

Four

"GENTLEMEN OF THE JURY,"
Assistant Prosecutor Oscar M. Springer opened for the
State of Michigan, "the defendant in this case is charged
with a serious crime—the offense of carnally knowing a

girl between the ages of 14 and 16 years. The alleged offense was committed in the City of Detroit, February last, upon the person of Bernice Bickle—a little girl, a mere child.

"Bernice, as you will see, is a beautiful girl. We shall establish that Prince Michael Mills first met her when she was playing the piano and singing at a revival meeting held in her uncle's home in Sarnia. And when the long-haired, bearded Prince first beheld her girlish figure and her ruby lips and her big blue eyes, we shall prove, his lustful and lascivious nature was aroused and he at once began to plan to catch his prey."

Watching the young state's attorney at work, Ben Purnell relaxed confidently in his seat. The last stage of his dethronement plot against the Israelite ruler was in good hands. Newspapers had mentioned this would be Springer's first really big case, certainly his first against an adversary as formidable as the famous Colonel John Atkinson; and even now, Prosecutor Samuel W. Burroughs was sitting in, shepherding the strategy, ready to help the moment he was needed.

Oscar Springer went on to point out that, from the beginning, it had been Prince Michael who'd forced the acquaintance—that Bernice, according to her own sworn statement, considered him a fraud and a funny-looking old man. Springer mentioned letters Mills had written to Bernice and her parents, money he'd sent in an attempt to bribe her to come to Detroit. He cited the mention of the Bickle girl in practically all of the Prince's business correspondence at the time, concluding that he obviously had Bernice on the brain. He went on with a detailed description of the various means of persuasion that had led to the actual seduction.

"He told her he had to sow seed in her body for the purpose of casting out evil. She refused. He asked if she was willing to obey him. No, she wept, not like that. He jumped up in a rage and shouted that the Lord would have a willing people. The next night he quoted the Bible to her by the hour, along with this Flying Roll book of his. He told her he was pure, and that to the pure all things were pure. He asked her then if she was not a little tease and pulled up her nightgown. She jerked it back down. A man of thirty-five, he kept this up until this child of fifteen could fight him off no longer.

"Naturally, for a girl of such tender years, intercourse was painful. When she flinched and cried, he ordered her to hold still and told her that once her seal was broken, intercourse would be a pleasure. Afterwards, she sobbed that she was bleeding. And what did the illustrious Prince say to this?

" 'Praise God,' he lectured her, 'for without the shedding of blood there is no remission of sin.'

"Why do I dwell on this point? Because, gentlemen of the jury, it is proof positive from the man's own lips that Bernice Bickle was a pure and chaste girl before she fell into this villainous clutches!

"Scientists tell us that we do not get more than half of the heat-producing properties from wood and coal; the other half is lost in ashes or goes off in gases and smoke. So it is with the prosecution of criminals. A great many of them escape by means of legal technicalities. There is not a lawyer in the entire State of Michigan able to discern a legal flyspeck quicker than the learned counsel for the defendant, the famed Colonel Atkinson. And so I must ask you, gentlemen of the jury, to be careful, to pay strict attention to the evidence as it comes in, and to pay attention only to the evidence. Thank you."

He turned to the bench where Circuit Judge Edward D. Kinne presided. "The People call Bernice Bickle."

As Ben Purnell watched the girl nervously take the stand and give a timid-voiced response to the oath, he saw quite obviously what had prompted Prince Mike. Bernice's lips weren't ruby, as Springer had insisted; they were, in fact, near-white and drawn very thin now. But her eyes were certainly big and blue. And her figure was far more than girlish.

"How old are you, Bernice?" the assistant prosecutor asked pleasantly.

"Fifteen." Her voice was low.

"When did you first meet the defendant, Michael Mills?"

"Last November."

"Where did you meet him?"

"At my uncle's house."

"I read you the opening line of a letter and ask if you can identify it: 'Well, dear Bernice, come to me. You are commanded by the living God of Abram, Isaac and Jacob to come and place yourself in Obedience to Michael, his son.'"

"He wrote that to me."

"Did he also write letters to your parents?"

"Yes."

"Were your parents followers of Michael Mills?"

"They were Israelites. He was the Prince. They showed me in my Bible where a great prince named Michael would stand up for the children of Israel and deliver them from trouble."

"That's in the Twelfth Chapter of the Book of Daniel, isn't it?"

"I don't remember."

"Did your parents then bring you to Detroit?"

"They sold our house and moved there."

"And you continued to live with them?"

"No. They found a house to rent and sent me to live at Prince Michael's house."

"In the house at thirty-seven Hamlin Avenue?"

"Yes, he said I had to come and be the tenth piece in the God-Head."

"I see. And how many pieces did the illustrious Prince have living with him at the time?"

"Objection!" Colonel Atkinson rose to his feet in righteous anger.

"The term is Prince Michael's, not mine, but I'll withdraw it," Oscar Springer shrugged. "Who else was there, Bernice?"

"Well . . . there was Mrs. Mills and Eliza Court." The

young girl counted on her fingers as she tried to remember. "And May Webster and Mary Ellen Rowlinson and Carrie Bendry and Emma Butler and Alice Court. That's all, I guess."

"How many beds were in that house?"

"Four."

"Just four? Each in a separate room?"

"Yes."

"Where did you sleep the first night?"

"With Mrs. Mills and May Webster."

"That was the twenty-first of December, was it not?"

"Yes."

"And the next night?"

"I slept with Mary Ellen Rowlinson."

"And the night after that?"

"They sent me to Prince Michael's room."

"Was he there?"

"Not at first. I went to bed early. Then he came in and sat down on the side of the bed."

"What did he say to you?"

"He talked about music and different things like that."

"What did he do after that?"

"He got undressed and got into bed."

"Did he say anything about Satan at that time?"

"Objection!" Colonel Atkinson boomed again. "Counsel is leading the witness!"

"Overruled," Judge Kinne decided.

"Did he say anything about Satan, Bernice?" the assistant prosecutor repeated.

"He said that Satan sowed tares, but the Son of Man sowed the good seed."

"The Son of Man?"

"He said he was the Son of Man and had been cleansed by the fire coming out of his hands and out of his hair."

"What did you say in answer to him?"

"I said no."

"Why did you say no?"

"Ojection!" Colonel Atkinson was on his feet once

more. "Counsel is calling for a conclusion on the part of the witness."

"Overruled," the judge told him.

"May I have an exception, your honor?"

"You have an appropriate exception."

"Now, Bernice," Horace Springer went on, "why did you say no?"

"Because I didn't understand it at all and I didn't want him to."

"When you refused to submit to him, what did he say to you? Did he say anything about obedience?"

Another objection was overruled.

"Yes, he said I had to obey him in everything."

"When was the next time you were sent to his room?"

"I think it was about three weeks after that."

"Did he quote the Bible to you extensively at that time?"

"Yes."

"Did he read to you from a book called *The Flying Roll?*"

"Yes."

"And did you submit to his desires?"

"No, I wouldn't do it."

"When was the next time you were ordered to sleep in Michael's room?"

"The twenty-first of February, I think."

"The twenty-first of February. You slept with Mills that night?"

"Yes, and with Eliza Court, too."

"The three of you? Who slept in the middle?"

"Objection!" Colonel Atkinson shouted. But not before Bernice had mumbled, "He did."

"What did the bearded Prince say to you at that time?"

"He said I was evil because I had been sleeping with Mrs. Mills and she was evil, and I'd caught it from her. He said I would have to sleep with him and Sister Eliza to get pure like they were. But after a while Sister Eliza got up and left."

"And what did Prince Michael say to you when Eliza Court was gone?"

"He said that by Obedience, Israel would be cleansed. He said that was the only way to be pure like him. He said he was as pure as Jesus was."

"And did the defendant, in fact, have carnal intercourse with you that night?"

"I told him no!" The girl was starting to cry a little. "I told him not to!"

"Just a few more questions, Bernice," the young state's attorney assured her. "Prior to that night, were you a chaste girl?"

"Yes."

"Had you ever had intercourse with anyone previously?" Springer repeated himself to establish the point firmly.

"No."

"Did the defendant himself say to you that you could always tell a virgin by the seal and that your seal had never been broken?"

"Yes."

"Did you call out for help when he hurt you?"

"I was afraid to. I was afraid he'd kill me. He said I had to choose what I wanted, life or death. He said the Lord would have only a willing people and all others would be burned alive."

"And he had carnal intercourse with you again after that?"

"Yes."

"And you were taken into protective custody by the police on March twenty-eighth, and have been living at the Woodbridge Station since that time?"

"Yes."

"I now show you two written statements and ask if these are your own statements, made of your own free will and signed without the offering of any inducements?"

"Yes, they are."

"Your honor, I offer these in evidence as People's exhibits A and B. No more questions."

Colonel John Atkinson rose and studied the two exhibits for a long time while the girl waited fearfully in the witness chair. From his seat in the second row, Ben Purnell watched the chief defense attorney carefully. He'd seen this famous criminal lawyer several times before, even talked to him briefly in offering himself as a character witness. The colonel was a very shrewd man, Ben had realized then. The colonel had sensed instantly that this redheaded overly sincere character couldn't be trusted, and he'd declined the offer.

"Who asked you to make this last statement, Bernice?" Atkinson's voice was gentle and disarming.

"I told the other girls about it. They said I'd better write it down. I wrote it myself."

"Now, Bernice, didn't you sign still another statement before either of these was made?"

"Another one? Oh . . . yes."

"Your honor." The colonel turned to the bench. "I demand that the prosecution produce that earlier statement."

Oscar Springer rose to his feet. "We're quite willing to do so, your honor, even to offer it in evidence . . . with, of course, the privilege of examining this witness on its contents." He handed over a sheet of paper to be marked People's Exhibit C. Colonel Atkinson took his time reading it.

"Did you write this, Bernice?" he finally asked, softly.

"Yes."

"Did you sign it?"

"So it seems you changed your story entirely while being held at Woodbridge Station. Originally, you swore there had been nothing wrong between you and the defendant."

"Prince Michael told me to. He said an oath didn't mean anything, because he was like a Catholic priest, and he could make it all right with God."

"Your witness." All at once, the Colonel turned and went back to the defendant's table.

This was an abrupt shock—to the young state's attorney, to the jury, to the entire crowded courtroom.

Ben Purnell edged forward on his seat in surprise. For the great Colonel Atkinson to drop his examination on such an unfavorable note, after making little attempt to shake the girl's story, seemed incredible. Something tricky was shaping up here.

Oscar Springer cautiously began his redirect questioning on the subject of Bernice's earlier statement.

"Bernice, you told the colonel that when I first talked to you at police headquarters you denied there was anything wrong because Prince Michael told you to, because he said he could make it all right with God for you to lie. Was there any other reason why you denied having intimate relations with him?"

"He said he'd put the handcuffs on me and lock me up like he did Mrs. Mills one time."

"I see. Now the colonel has insinuated that someone told you to make your statements. Did anyone, since you've been confined in Woodbridge Station, ever ask you to make any statement that was not true in every sense of the word?"

"No."

"Thank you. No more questions."

"Just one moment, young lady!" Colonel John Atkinson rose suddenly and moved quickly to the witness chair, stopping Bernice as she started to leave. His voice had changed completely. It now had the same crisp deadliness as the crack of a whip. "You have mentioned, and the state's attorney has repeated, that Prince Michael considered his office to be something like that of a Catholic priest. Did you, by any chance, make confession in the Israelite colony, the way the Catholics do?"

"Yes," the girl admitted, puzzled now.

"As a matter of fact, you have to write out an accounting of all your sins before you can join the colony, don't you?"

Bernice could only nod.

"Please speak up, young lady." Judge Kinne prompted her.

"Yes." Her voice trembled.

"Now, Bernice, when you confessed your sins upon

first entering the colony, didn't you admit doing what you called 'bad things' with two different male persons?"

The girl couldn't answer. She looked trapped and helpless.

"Didn't you admit having connection with two different male persons before ever coming to Detroit?"

Sobbing hysterically now, the girl finally choked out an admission.

"So you lied to us!" The colonel snapped at her, and she winced at each word. "So you weren't really chaste when you came to the colony!"

"I don't know!" Bernice cried. "I don't know!"

"Your honor!" Assistant Prosecutor Springer rushed up to the bench. "If any so-called confession exists in writing, as counsel claims, let him produce it and let it be admitted in evidence. This is the cheapest sort of courtroom trick I've ever seen. After what this girl has endured at the hands of that—"

"Your honor," Colonel Atkinson protested, "other names than that of this witness are involved in that confession. And, I might add, other sins. None of which have any bearing on this case. I have established the only pertinent point through examination of this witness."

Judge Kinne motioned them both to the bench, where they argued the point out of hearing of the jury and the audience. Ben Purnell sat stunned by this new development. He'd known of the written confessions that were required for admission to the colony, of course. He'd written one out himself, filling it with vague meaningless generalities. But the colonel's unrefuted suggestions about what the Bickel girl's confession had contained were simply impossible. Whispers about the blood on the sheets in God-House that morning had circulated throughout the New and Latter House of Israel. Ben had never fully realized before that the girl's chastity, or lack of it, had any particular bearing on the law under which Mike Mills was being tried. But now, remembering how the state's attorney has stressed the point in opening, he realized this was extremely important.

Judge Kinne finally made his ruling. The defense would not be required to produce the alleged confession. The prosecution could probe its contents by examination of the witness. Bernice was still crying and Oscar Springer did his best to calm her as he began the difficult task.

"Why did you write this so-called confession which the colonel is so afraid to produce, Bernice? Did you write it of your own free will?"

"No," the girl sobbed, "Sister Eliza made me do it."

"I see. How long ago was it when the 'bad things' in this alleged confession were done?"

"I don't remember." The girl was back on the brink of hysteria.

"Wasn't it a number of years ago, Bernice?"

"I guess so."

"Can you remember how many years ago, Bernice?"

"No," she choked.

"But you must have been just a little girl then. You're hardly more than a mere child right now. These 'male persons' the colonel talked about—weren't they just little boys?"

Bernice nodded, but her answer was inaudible. She was breaking down completely now, coming apart inside, choking and shuddering as she cried.

"Now tell us what you did with the little boys, Bernice," Springer urged her, fighting hard to get out a few more precious answers before she collapsed. "Don't be afraid. Weren't the little boys just fooling around with you?"

"I don't know!" she gasped. "I don't know what you mean!"

"Was . . . was there any penetration of you by the little boys?" the assistant prosecutor prodded her desperately.

Her voice entirely out of control, Bernice shook her head, then nodded, then twisted her head about meaningless. And Oscar Springer was forced to give up.

"All right, Bernice," he soothed her. "All right. It's all

over now." He turned to the bench. "No more questions, your honor."

"I think we've made sufficient progress for today." Judge Kinne had a pained expression on his face as he adjourned the court.

Benjamin Franklin Purnell was deeply worried. His dethronement plot was in serious trouble. If the girl's chastity was a crucial point of law and the state's attorney was able to do no more to erase the doubts Colonel Atkinson had planted, Prince Mike might very well walk out of the courthouse a free man as a result of a directed verdict of not guilty.

The more he thought about Bernice Bickle and her alleged written confession, the more Ben was sure the defense lawyer was shrewdly misreading it. Where would that confession be now? In the colonel's possession? Probably not. Atkinson wouldn't be carrying it about or leaving it in his Detroit office and risking a charge of suppressing evidence. Would the Prince or Eliza Court be carrying it? Once again, probably not. The chance of losing it would be too great. No, Bernice's confession was most certainly secreted away in some remote corner of God-House.

If he had to stay up the entire night searching, Ben Purnell promised himself, he was going to find it.

Five

At THE OPENING of the second day's proceedings in the trial of Prince Mike, the prosecution called a young Flying Roller woman named May Webster to the stand. Bernice Bickle was not in the courtroom. The morning newspapers had rumored that she'd been sent to a rest home.

"How old are you, Miss Webster?" Oscar Springer asked.

"Twenty-seven," she admitted.

"And how long have you known the defendant, Michael Mills?"

"About four years."

"Where did you first meet him?"

"At my sister's home in Toronto."

"How long have you been living with Prince Michael in the house at thirty-seven Hamlin Avenue?"

"Since November."

"Who else was living there besides you and the Prince?"

"Eliza Court, Rosetta Mills, Emma Butler, Carrie Bendry, Alice Court, Mary Ellen Rowlinson and Bernice Bickle."

"When did Bernice first come to the house?"

"On the twenty-first of December."

"Where did she sleep?"

"With Rosetta and me, the first night."

"And the second?"

"With Mary Ellen Rowlinson."

"And the third?"

"I don't know."

"Do you know if Bernice ever slept with Prince Michael?"

"Yes. There was a night when she slept with Michael and Eliza both. I remember because Eliza left and came down to sleep with us. I made the bed in Michael's room that morning and there was blood on the sheet."

"Do you know if anyone else saw that sheet?"

"I showed to to Eliza. She said, 'Hallelujah! Now that Obedience has been obtained, Israel will be gathered!' "

In the middle of the row of bearded, long-haired Pillars, Ben Purnell had to catch himself to keep from laughing, to keep from nodding in satisfaction. The state's attorney was recovering nicely from the surprise set-back of the day before and was wading in boldly with a new attack, once again stressing the essential legal question of virginity.

Ben's eyes were swollen. He'd been struggling to stay awake as he'd waited for Judge Kinne to enter, for the proceedings to resume. All through the hours of darkness, he'd probed about the Hamlin Avenue house with a candle, hunting that crucial piece of paper. He'd found enough interesting material to support a skillful blackmailer indefinitely, and he'd appropriated a good share of it for use in his future bid for power. But nowhere had he seen the confession of Bernice Bickle.

"How did you come to tell about occurrences at Prince Michael's house after you were taken to the Woodbridge Station?" the assistant prosecutor was asking the witness. "Were any inducements offered to you?"

"No, there was no inducement."

Oscar Springer turned to the bench. "Your honor, in a statement made to the police, this witness said that the proceedings at Michael Mills' house were all right because it was to cleanse their bodies. I'd like to have her explain to this jury exactly what she meant by that."

"I'll allow it," Judge Kinne ruled.

"What did you refer to, Miss Webster?"

"Sleeping with Prince Michael."

"You said that you came to the station prepared to deny everything. Did you feel that you were still under the Prince's power?"

"Objection!" Colonel John Atkinson thundered.

"I was."

"Please don't answer until the objection is disposed of, young lady," Judge Kinne told her. "Overruled. Allow the answer to stand."

"Your witness," Oscar Springer told the colonel.

As Atkinson walked to the stand, Ben Purnell watched him apprehensively.

"Isn't it true, Miss Webster," he opened cross-examination, "that at first you denied having relations with Michael Mills?"

"Yes."

"Where were you living when you decided to change your story?"

"At the police station."

"You've been living there ever since March twenty-eighth?"

"Yes."

"Now isn't it true that Detectives Shoemaker and Lombard have had free access to your room, that they've taken you for walks and even to Belle Isle on occasion, that they've spent many hours in your room, playing checkers, smoking in your presence, throughout this period during which you changed your story?"

May Webster admitted this was true.

"Incidentally, how late have these men stayed in your room at the Woodbridge Station? As late as, say, eleven?"

"Sometimes. Not very often."

"As late as midnight?"

"Never that late."

"That's all, I think."

"A few more questions." Oscar Springer rose for redirect. "Did the defendant call a meeting of all the pieces in his God-Head about a week before his arrest?"

"Sister Eliza called it. She said Prince Michael wanted to talk to us."

"And what did the illustrious Prince have to say at that meeting?"

"He made us swear we'd say no if anybody asked anything."

"If anyone asked about carnal misconduct on his part?"

"Yes."

"Thank you, May." The state's attorney turned away, and Colonel Atkinson hurried back in before the girl could rise.

"Do you believe in God, Miss Webster?" he asked softly.

"I don't know," she shook her head. "I don't even know, any more."

"Do you believe in the Bible, the Bible upon which you took an oath to tell the truth?"

"I don't know if I believe anything, any more."

"Did Dr. Daniel La Ferte and Dr. Charles A. Devendorf examine you and Bernice for evidence of sexual intercourse when you were first brought to the Woodbridge Station?"

"There were two doctors who examined us. I don't know their names."

"Tell us about it."

"I don't know what there is to tell. They examined us and it hurt. Bernice cried out several times."

"Didn't anyone tell you these doctors found no evidence of sexual intercourse?"

"Objection!" Oscar Springer shouted. "Your honor, counsel knows full well that a negative result on a vaginal-slide sperm test warrants no such conclusion."

"Of course," Judge Kinne nodded. "Sustained."

"That's all." Colonel Atkinson went back to his seat beside the bearded Prince and his cross-faced Spiritual Affinity.

"The People call Mary Ellen Rowlinson," Oscar Springer announced.

Once again, Ben Purnell had to admire Mike Mills' taste in women. This Flying Roller girl had an enticing walk even in the prim clothing provided for her appearance here.

"How old are you, Mary Ellen?" the assistant prosecutor asked.

"Nineteen."

"When did you first meet the defendant, Prince Michael Mills?"

"Last November."

"Where did you meet him?"

"At a revival meeting in Ontario."

"When did you come to live in his house at thirty-seven Hamlin Avenue?"

"On December twenty-second."

"Did you come there of your own free will?"

"No, my parents sent me."

"By the way, what virtue were you supposed to represent as a piece in the God-Head?"

"Temperance."

"Who else lived in that house at that time?"

"Prince Michael, Sister Eliza, Mrs. Mills, May Webster,

Alice Court, Emma Butler, Bernice Bickle. And there was a girl named Armstrong there for a while. I never knew her first name."

"Where did you sleep the first night?"

"With Bernice."

"The second?"

"With May Webster and Mrs. Mills."

"The third?"

"With Prince Michael."

"Do you know if Bernice ever slept with Prince Michael?"

"I know for sure she did on February twenty-first."

"Were you in the room?"

"No."

"Did you see the bedclothes afterward?"

"No."

"Did you hear Prince Michael say anything about the blood on those bedclothes?"

"No. But before that I heard him say that Bernice was very rebellious and that the spirit of God would not plead with her much longer."

"How did you come to leave Prince Michael's house?"

"I got a letter out to my father telling him what was going on. He came and got me with a policeman."

"When was this?"

"Early in March."

"Thank you, Mary Ellen." Oscar Springer turned to the colonel. "Your witness."

Atkinson took his time approaching the witness stand. "Tell me, Mary Ellen. Didn't you swear out a warrant in Recorder's Court of the City of Detroit charging both Michael K. Mills and Eliza Court with rape?"

"Yes. When my father first came and got me."

"But you subsequently dropped those charges."

"I wanted to go home. I didn't want to stay in Detroit any longer."

"I can understand that, Mary Ellen. But didn't you come back to Detroit on April twelfth and haven't you been living at the Woodbridge Station ever since?"

"Well, I wanted to clear my name."

"Clear your name? In what manner was your name attacked, and by whom?"

"I don't know."

"Tell me, Mary Ellen. Are you also going to claim you were a chaste girl before you went to live at Prince Michael's?" the colonel sneered.

"Objection!" Oscar Springer shouted.

"Sustained!" Judge Kinne glared at Colonel Atkinson.

"No more questions." The defense attorney smiled.

As his last witness, Assistant Prosecutor Springer called Police Chief Christopher C. Starkweather to the stand. Under examination, the officer related that the defendant was brought to the Woodbridge Station for questioning on the evening of April 11, that he was confronted with the statement made by Bernice Bickle, and that he did not deny the charges.

"Do you remember his exact words?" Oscar Springer asked.

"Yes. He said, 'I will neither affirm nor deny it. I am not responsible for it. I will not attempt to justify myself.' "

Under cross-examination, Chief Starkweather admitted arresting all of the people he found at the Hamlin Street house, in spite of the fact that he had warrants only for Michael Mills and Eliza Court. He also admitted giving audience to a citizens' committee and assigning a Captain Wyler to investigate their charges that the Flying Roller colony was a menace to public morals.

The prosecution then rested its case, and Colonel Atkinson objected violently to this. Other witnesses had been named in the original information supplied to the court—Rosetta Mills, Alice Court, Emma Butler, Detectives J. L. Lombard and H. E. Shoemaker. The colonel demanded that the People produce these witnesses. Oscar Springer argued that Mrs. Mills was living somewhere in Canada and was unobtainable, that the others were available, but that an irrefutable case, in his opinion, had been established without the use of further witnesses. Judge Edward D. Kinne ruled that if Colonel Atkinson wished to examine the others, he could call them as defense witnesses. A brief recess was held so the colonel might talk with Alice Court and Emma Butler, who were being held in the judge's chambers.

Upon returning, Colonel John Atkinson opened for the defense by characterizing Michael K. Mills as a victim of religious prejudice. And yet the Israelite faith, he insisted, differed little from other Christian faiths. The Israelites believed in baptism like the Baptists, in confession like the Catholics. They believed in the Trinity. In fact, he claimed, there was only one essential difference. Most Christians believed in the second coming of Christ. The Israelites believed that the time of this coming was close at hand.

Prince Michael, the colonel insisted, was here in court only because of a gigantic intricate plot hatched by certain Detroit real estate interests and certain North Side merchants. Because of their long hair and beards, it was thought the Israelites would depress real estate values in the Hamlin Avenue area by causing other residents to move out. Because the Israelites were vegetarians who bought their few necessities from wholesalers, local merchants resented their coming and were also involved in the plot against Prince Michael.

Colonel Atkinson went on to promise that he'd prove that the Detroit police and Detroit newspapers actively joined in this conspiracy, that all of the girls who testified against the Prince were paid to do so. He repeated his earlier insistence that Bernice Bickle was not a chaste girl before coming into the colony.

As his first witness, the colonel called Detective Judson Lombard to the stand. Under questioning, Lombard admitted that Mrs. Rosetta Mills had hesitated for a long time before making a criminal complaint against her husband and that members of a citizens' committee had urged her on. Oscar Springer declined to cross-examine.

The colonel then called Detective Henry Shoemaker.

"When was the first time you entered the house at thirty-seven Hamlin Avenue?"

"March second of this year. I went up with Mr. Rowlinson to get Mary Ellen out of there."

"Did you attend a citizens' meeting held at Brown's Hall to discuss means of ridding Detroit of the Israelites?"

"I did."

"Was Mrs. Rosetta Mills present at that meeting?"

"She was."

"Is it true that when she was asked to make a criminal complaint against the defendant, she twice refused before finally doing so?"

"It is."

"Have you visited these girls at the Woodbridge Station regularly, often in the evening?"

"I have."

"Have you sometimes stayed as late as eleven?"

"On a very few occasions."

"Your witness," Colonel Atkinson told Oscar Springer.

The young assistant prosecutor merely rose from his chair. "Just one question. Has there ever been anything in any way improper in your relations with these girls? Or, to the best of your knowledge, anything improper done by any other member of the police department?"

"Of course not!" Detective Shoemaker snorted. "There was a police matron present at all times."

"Thank you." The state's attorney looked at the defense lawyer, shook his head sadly, then sat back down.

Very suddenly, Colonel John Atkinson pulled his second major surprise out of the hat, a surprise almost as shocking as his suggestions about Bernice's confession had been. One by one, he called Bernice Bickle's parents, William and Elizabeth Bickle, to the stand as character witnesses for the defendant, Michael Mills. Both professed their trust and belief in their Prince, in his immaculate character, in his purity of conduct. Both denounced their daughter hotly, branding her a habitual and imaginative liar and swearing they'd never speak to her again.

While the entire courtroom sat stunned in silence, Assistant Prosecutor Springer fought valiantly to shake their righteous smug-faced testimony. But it was hopeless. By this time, they'd convinced themselves they were telling the truth. The best the young state's attorney could do was to show the jury what blind unreasoning fanatics they were.

On that note, Judge Kinne adjourned for the day.

From where Ben Purnell sat, things weren't going at all well. The reasonable doubt that the jury needed had been planted by the colonel's claim that Bernice had been no virgin when she first came to the God-House. That doubt had been enlarged and hardened by the testimony of the Bickles. If it remained in the mind of a single juror, the Prince would go free and return to rule the Israelite colony. And all of Ben's elaborate plans would be destroyed, all of his intricate plotting and scheming wasted.

He had to find that confession.

Six

ONCE AGAIN the day in Washtenaw County Circuit Court opened with a Flying Roller girl in the witness chair. This time it was young Emma Butler, called by the defense.

"How long have you lived in the house at thirty-seven Hamlin Avenue?" Colonel John Atkinson asked her.

"For several months now."

"Have you ever seen or heard anything in the slightest way improper in the conduct of the defendant, Michael Mills?"

"No," the girl swore. "Nothing."

"There has been testimony of an alleged meeting taking place just prior to the defendant's arrest, a meeting at which he supposedly ordered the girls to give false stories to the police. Will you tell us about this?"

"There wasn't any such meeting. There wasn't ever anything like that."

In cross-examination, Assistant Prosecutor Springer was unable to shake the girl's testimony.

Colonel Atkinson next called two character witnesses named Joseph Dickinson and Hobart Gray. Both testified that they'd known Mills for many years. They described him as honest, sober, moral and religious, stating they'd never heard a single indecent expression from his lips.

The best young Oscar Springer could do in cross-examination was to bring out the admission that they hadn't seen Mike Mills at all since he'd become an Israelite.

Three more character witnesses followed—Joseph Daley, Edward Durand and Samuel Taylor—all long-haired bearded Flying Rollers. Each swore fervently that Prince Michael was a saint. The state's attorney was able to make no dent in their testimony, but he was able to make their blind fanaticism clear to the jury.

The last defense witness was a man named Flavius Brooke. Under the colonel's skillful guidance, he described a number of the citizens' meetings that had been held and read aloud a number of articles from the Detroit papers, articles with headings like A BESTIAL RELIGION, A HUMAN DEVIL or LONG-HAIRED PRINCE OF DARKNESS. He mentioned that money had been collected for the girls on a number of occasions.

In cross-examination, Oscar Springer managed to establish that the total amount of money collected for the girls was mere pin money, that Bernice Bickle, for example, had received only $2.06 for a few necessities while living at the police station, and that these donations had come from reputable established churches.

"Your honor," Colonel Atkinson rose to address Judge Kinne after Flavius Brooke was dismissed from the chair. "I wish to express my sincere regret that the defendant's religion forbids him to testify in his own behalf. The defense now rests."

Groans of disappointment and then catcalls came from the crowded courtroom. The audience had been looking forward to watching Prince Mike undergo questioning.

The judge dutifully quieted the outburst. And Assistant Prosecutor Springer then stepped forward to sum up for the State of Michigan.

"The counsel for the defendant made many allegations as to what he would prove here," the young state's attorney began, "among other things, finding fault with the police and charging them with perjury and suborning perjury. He insisted over and over again that he would prove the existence of a vast conspiracy against the defendant, a conspiracy in which the police, the press, the merchants and real estate brokers, the citizens and the churches of the north side of Detroit were all involved. I ask you now, has he proven anything of the kind?"

Oscar Springer went on to attack the claims of the defense in a sound but somewhat routine manner. The jury and the audience listened attentively. But they wanted more fireworks. Disappointment hung in the air.

Then, very abruptly, the assistant prosecutor was waving a sheet of paper.

"The counsel for the defendant also insinuated that young Bernice Bickle was not a virgin at the time this crime was committed. He accused her of 'having connection' with other men and threatened her with a mysterious confession she'd made, taking advantage of the fact that she'd broken down under the ordeal of testifying here, to plant doubts about her chastity in your minds. Upon being pressed to produce this alleged confession as evidence, he ducked out on a convenient legal technicality. Well, I have this so-called confession that Eliza Court, who sits there at the side of the defendant, forced this child to write—this incriminating document the defense was afraid to produce. And when I read it to you, you'll see—"

"Objection!" Colonel Atkinson shouted with all the strength in his lungs. "Your honor, that document was obtained by an illegal search and cannot be admitted in evidence. Furthermore, it is a confidence protected by law. The names of the innocent are involved here!"

"Including the name of innocent little Bernice Bickle!" Oscar Springer shouted back at him.

"Gentlemen! Gentlemen!" Judge Kinne slammed down his gavel again and again as the angry words of the lawyers rose above the roar of the crowd. "Approach the bench!"

While the attorneys argued the point in a huddle with the judge and the courtroom hummed with anticipation, Michael Mills and Eliza Court whispered together, and the fear on their faces was clear for all to read. Behind them, in their row of supporters, Benjamin Franklin Purnell sat with his features frozen in haughty righteousness. But, once again, when Judge Kinne finally ruled that the state's attorney could read the confession, the strange eyes framed by the long red-gold hair and beard were practically laughing out loud.

He'd finally found the right paper, hidden away in a remote corner of God-House. Once he'd read it, the reason the defense was keeping it out of evidence was obvious. Before the proceedings began that morning, he'd slipped it to a prosecution aide.

"'I confess before the God of the Living,'" the assistant prosecutor now read, "'that I have sinned in thought and word and deed. Six or seven years ago I did bad things with a boy named Elias Jones and my brother Frank because they threatened me that the boogieman would catch me. I stole money from my mother's purse and five cents from my father's pocket. When my mother scolded me I made faces and called her names behind her back. I cut my hair in the front and then denied it up and down. I teased my cousin until she got angry and then talked about her behind her back. I talked about Mrs. Redfern and called her a bitch and Lottie a little slut. I said I didn't like Sister Eliza Court because she is too cross-looking. I said I would not be an Israelite because they look silly with their hair hanging down. About a week before I came here, I was asked what church my parents belonged to. Because there was so much bad talk about the Israelites, I said Methodist.

This is all I know about and I am sorry and pray that God will forgive me. Bernice Bickle.' "

The courtroom audience sat in shocked silence, then broke out muttering. Angry stares burned down on Mike Mills and his Spiritual Affinity and his attorney from every direction. Oscar Springer waited just long enough to let the words sink in, then went on explosively.

"These, gentlemen of the jury, are the sins little Bernice has committed! This is the confession Colonel Atkinson has talked about and made such a great point of in attempting to convince you she was not a virgin when she fell into the defendant's clutches. She was seven or eight years old! The typical sex play of a little girl with her brother and a little neighbor boy! The games of children! Playing Doctor, most likely! This is what the colonel calls 'having connection with a male person,' blistering his lips with shame in trying to drag her down in infamy." He paused and pointed at the long-haired Prince. "To protect a man like this in his villainy! To shield a man like this in his crimes!"

He shook his head slowly. "Gentlemen of the jury, think of the awful things little Bernice told us. Nothing could prevail upon him to stop. She prayed, she cried, she pleaded, she protested .... and in all of the eminent speeches of the great Colonel Atkinson, including the one he is certain to make when I finish, nowhere will you find as much eloquence as in that simple answer she gave here—'I told him not to. I told him to stop.'

"She could say no more. She was powerless, a lamb in the hands of the wolf, at his mercy in his den of infamy, wickedness and disgrace.

"If there is a man on this jury who has a daughter, who has watched her as she came from the cradle and began to toddle and then to walk and then to run and meet him when he came home at night . . . if there is a man on this jury who loves his little girl as I love mine . . . he cannot help but feel about this case as I feel about it. My daughter is dearer to me than the blood that flows through my heart this second. And if anybody should be guilty of committing a crime like this upon her . . . the Lord have mercy upon him . . . I wouldn't.

"Gentlemen of the jury, do your duty and do it quickly. Send little Bernice Bickle forth as a pure girl and a lady, not a harlot and a prostitute. Let that child go out of this court, not branded forever, but with a verdict that will give her . . . justice . . . simply that and nothing more . . . and then go home to your families. I thank you."

The courtroom applauded and cheered wildly, while the gavel of Judge Kinne slammed down again and again.

Just as the young assistant prosecutor had predicted, Colonel Atkinson rose to the occasion with superb skill and eloquence. He repeated his claim that a gigantic conspiracy against the defendant had been plotted, that the witnesses had been bribed, that the police had taken part in the plot and had taken indecent liberties with the girls while holding them at the Woodbridge Station. He cited the admissions he'd won from the two detectives, and the testimony of Flavius Brooke about the citizens' meetings and the raising of funds. Finally he launched into a brilliant passage comparing Prince Michael to Christ and the Bickle girl to Barabbas.

"The mob is screaming, 'Crucify him and give us Barabbas!' The newspapers, the curious and unthinking who crowd this courtroom, the human refuse on the lawn outside—all are demanding that you clear the name of an appealing little thief who has been bribed to commit perjury, by nailing up on the cross a just man who has been guilty of nothing more than practising the religion he preaches!"

But it was no use. Puncturing the doubts about Bernice Bickle's chastity, the introduction of the childishly innocent confession had already decided the case. There was no applause for the colonel's eloquence when he finally ended his arguments.

Judge Edward Kinne then charged the jury. He mentioned that the Bickle girl's virginity, or lack of it, was a crucial point of the offense with which the defendant was charged. But he also mentioned that the childish sex-play of a seven- or eight-year-old girl was not to be considered in determining her chastity.

"Seldom are courts of justice called upon to investigate human affairs so painful and distressing, if true," he announced. "If such a crime has been committed, as the people assert, public justice demands a prompt and complete vindication."

The jury gave him just that, remaining out only five minutes before bringing back a verdict of guilty.

The courtroom audience broke out in the loudest and longest burst of cheering yet. The judge made no move to quiet the demonstration, but merely waited patiently until it wore itself out, then gave Prince Michael K. Mills the maximum sentence—five years at hard labor in Jackson State Prison.

"Take me, too!" Eliza Court shrieked as a deputy sheriff led the deposed Prince away. "Take me with him! Let me bear his cross! Let me share his torment!"

The deputies dragged her back, kicking and scratching.

Benjamin Franklin Purnell had been privileged to witness the vengeance that awaited false prophets, the swift and inexorable wrath of the State of Michigan. The lesson should have been clear and obvious.

But Ben Purnell hadn't learned it. His only thought, as he left that Ann Arbor courtroom, was that the path to power was open now, that the throne was empty and waiting.

Seven

IT WAS earliest morning—the hushed moment just before sunrise. In the stately parlor of God-House, surrounded by lavish furnishings that contrasted strangely with the drab Hamlin Avenue rooming house district beyond the unshaded window, the Pillars of

Israel sat in pious meditation. Heads were bowed. Eyes were closed. Like a small boy mischievously and impatiently glancing about him while a blessing is being asked, the Pillar with the red-gold hair and beard was staring briefly and calculatingly at each of the solemn faces.

This meeting was a daily ritual, called for the purpose of offering prayers for the speedy return of their imprisoned Prince, the martyred Michael Mills, for the righting of the terrible wrong done him, for the eternal damnation of all those responsible. But Benjamin Franklin Purnell was carefully sizing up his fellow Pillars, waiting for exactly the right moment.

With a loud sudden groan he slumped down in his chair. Eyes came open. Heads were lifted. Ben Purnell's arms flopped from his lap and hung limply. His chin rested on his chest. A soft moan, almost inaudible, came from somewhere deep inside him. Then another, like far-off cries in the night. He shuddered spasmodically, his entire body shaking.

Startled from their prayers, the other Pillars hurried to help him. But they jumped back cautiously as his seizure grew steadily more violent. Loud groans and fits of choking came on in a rush. Trails of saliva ran down from the corners of his mouth and the sounds he was making became animal sounds. Roaring and howling, coughing thunderously, he kept the others at a respectful distance, like hounds cringing back around a snarling bear brought to bay.

Abruptly, the sounds cut off. His shivering stopped. His head came slowly up from his chest, and a calm angelic smile was on his face as he stared straight ahead. His eyes were closed tightly. His lips scarcely seemed to move as an echoing resonant voice began intoning, a voice that filled the room and seemed weirdly disconnected with the stricken mortal from whom it came.

"The sceptre shall not depart from Judah, nor a lawgiver from between his feet, until Shiloh come, and unto him shall the gathering of the people be."

"The Spirit!" someone whispered excitedly. "The Spirit has descended and lit upon him!"

"*A lamb stood on the mount, and with him a hundred and forty-four thousand, which were redeemed from the earth, and in their mouth was found no guile, for they are without fault before the throne.*"

"Praise be!" another whisper came.

"*That there should be time no longer. Seal up those things which the seven thunders uttered and write them not. But in the days of the voice of the seventh angel, when he shall begin to sound, the mystery of God should be finished, as he hath declared to his servants the prophets.*"

"Amen!" a chorus of whispers added.

Ben Purnell's eyes opened abruptly. He stared in surprise at the Pillars who clustered about him.

"I am the Seventh Angelic Messenger!" he announced, seemingly as startled by this revelation as everyone else in the room.

There was a long hush of shocked silence. Then cross-faced Eliza Court finally spoke up.

"That's blasphemy!" she hissed in the heavy quiet. "Prince Michael is the Seventh Messenger!"

"Michael Keyfor Mills is an imposter, a secret servant of the forces of evil, a Son of Dan, a scorpion we have wrongly harbored at our breasts!" Ben Purnell shouted, rising to his feet in righteous indignation. "The mark of the beast was written upon his forehead. I am the true Seventh Divine Messenger. My destiny is revealed to me. I am Shiloh, the chosen leader of the Lost Tribes of Israel. I shall unite Judah and Israel. I shall rule Jezreel. I shall shepherd the In-gathering. I shall guide the faithful to eternal life. Fire and brimstone await those who doubt me."

"Blasphemy!" Eliza screeched.

"Fire and brimstone!" he threatened her. "I am the light and the life, alpha and omega, the beginning and the end." His voice grew suddenly calm and soothing, almost hypnotic. "The Millennium is close at hand now.

Everlasting rest. Everlasting peace. We shall live and reign for a thousand years." His voice rose to a thunderous roar once again. "But whosoever is not found written in the book of life shall be cast into the lake of fire! Follow me or burn in everlasting damnation!"

Ben was gambling everything on this moment, and he felt the same spine-tingling chill a man might feel watching a roulette wheel spin while his life's savings rode on the numbered table. But even so, like any born gambler, he was enjoying himself immensely.

Nearly three years had gone by since that Ann Arbor jury had brought in their verdict and the crowded courtroom had cheered them for it. Watching the dethroned Prince being led off in handcuffs, Ben Purnell had considered his own future bright and clear. It would be necessary for the Flying Rollers to present an appearance of absolute piety and humility to the outside world for some time, of course. If the slightest breath of scandal came to the Detroit colony while public feeling still ran high and hot, while the newspapers were still hungry for more juicy details of harem-keeping, the New and Latter House of Israel would fall. On the other hand, if the Israelite colony could merely be kept intact until the press and public lost interest, Ben reckoned he'd have little trouble in taking over.

But Ben Purnell had soon discovered that he'd reckoned without Eliza Court, the senior member of the Prince's abolished harem. Eliza had campaigned energetically among the Israelites to raise enough money to appeal Mills' conviction, to carry the fight all the way to the Supreme Court of Michigan. Ben had found this amusing, especially when the higher court had upheld the Prince's conviction. Eliza had then pestered every public official from the warden up to the governor with her shrill demand that she be allowed to share her beloved Divine Messenger's prison cell, a demand that was of course refused. Ben had found this amusing, too. But then Eliza Court had suddenly announced that Michael Mills had appointed her to rule the Israelites during his absence, producing an edict from the Prince confirming this, even insisting that she be addressed as Princess Michael in the future. To Ben Purnell, this was no longer amusing.

Ben had been baffled for some time in his search for a means of combating this threat to his plans. Still pretending loyalty to the imprisoned Prince, he'd swallowed his revulsion and made a few subtle advances toward the hatchet-faced new Princess, hinting that they needed each other now that the Divine Messenger, the joy and light of both their lives, was no longer here to comfort them. But he'd found Eliza Court singularly immune to his charm, fanatically devoted to Mike Mills.

Ben had then attempted to discredit the Princess among the Little People of the Israelite colony, spreading a number of vicious rumors about her. Eliza had been the real cause of Prince Mike's downfall, Ben had whispered to Mary and others equally gullible. Eliza had secretly plotted with real estate brokers and merchants and other enemies in the outside world to bring about the Prince's arrest so she could claim the throne for herself. But this approach had also failed.

Ben Purnell had grown desperate. With Prince Mike's prison sentence already half served, Ben was no nearer his goal of ruling the Israelites than he'd been in his first days in the colony. Once the Prince returned, the chance would most likely be lost forever. There had seemed only one course left—claiming Divine guidance.

But Johanna Southcott had specified that there would be only seven Angelic Messengers. He could hardly get away with proclaiming himself the eighth. He had to gamble on denouncing Prince Mike as an imposter.

He'd made careful preparations for his revelation, secretly practising for long hours before a mirror. He'd known full well that he'd have to be convincing enough to win over a dozen of the Prince's most faithful lieutenants.

At the prayer meeting on the morning of March 12, 1895, he'd picked his moment and made his pitch.

"You have worshipped the spawn of Satan!" he raved.

"Could a true Angelic Messenger lie rotting behind cold prison walls without the seven thunders sounding and the flaming wrath of the Most High descending to avenge him? No! The false prophet shall be cast into the lake of fire, and all who are deceived by him and receive the mark of the beast in their foreheads shall not live again until the thousand years are done!"

"The Written Word tells us the Lord speaks in a small still voice," Eliza Court reminded the other Pillars. "Brother Benjamin has been bellowing like a mad bull!"

Wild-eyed he turned to face her, leveling one of his waving arms to point an accusing finger directly into her face.

"There she is!" he roared. "Mother of harlots and abominations of the earth, drunken with the blood of saints, the great whore that sitteth upon many waters. Babylon is her name!"

"Like a mad bull!" she repeated, facing him without flinching.

"Stand off for fear of her torment!" Ben warned the others. "Be not partakers of her sins and receive not of her plagues. For her sins have reached into Heaven and her plagues shall come in one day—death and mourning and famine—and she shall be utterly burned with fire."

"Foulness!" the Princess retorted. "Foulness and blasphemy!"

"Strong is the Lord God who judgeth her," Ben shouted, "and the kings of the earth, who have committed fornication and lived deliciously with her, shall bewail her and lament for her, when they shall see the smoke of her burning!"

"This is the scorpion Prince Michael had harbored!" Eliza pointed her own finger. "This is how our Prince's bounty and kindness have been rewarded."

The strange debate raged on throughout the entire morning. Other Flying Rollers joined in from time to time, but the argument consisted mostly of accusations and counter-accusations between Ben Purnell and Eliza Court. Finally, a little past noon, the Pillars decided to adjourn their meeting, to consider this claim carefully and to meet again to discuss it the next morning.

Like politicians scurrying to solicit and round up support during a recess at a nominating convention, the red-headed Pillar and the loyal champion of the imprisoned Prince worked all through the afternoon and far into the night, urging the other Pillars to back them, wooing them with impossible promises, even campaigning directly among the Little People. Ben Purnell was, of course, at a distinct disadvantage in this type of in-fighting. The burden of proof was definitely on him, but he had some ammunition for the fight he was making.

"The false prophet has feasted on the fruits of your labor," he shrewdly and correctly pointed out to the Flying Rollers. "You have sown but you have not reaped. By their fruits shall you know them. Do men gather grapes of thorns or figs of thistles? No, a corrupt tree bringeth evil fruits. And what has been the fruit of Mills' rule? You have gathered only strife. Your homes have been smashed. You have been stoned and whipped in the streets."

Ben Purnell mixed tough talk with the sweet, carefully sandwiching his threats of eternal fire and brimstone between glowing promises of eternal happiness and hints that the Millennium was very close at hand. He reminded many of the Israelites of the choicest bits of information from their confessions, the confessions he'd found while searching God-House when Mike Mills was on trial in Ann Arbor. It seemed to him that he was succeeding, that the Little People of the colony were being convinced. But he kept on pleading his cause relentlessly, preaching to all who would stand still a moment to listen. Not until the lights of the cluster of rooming houses where the Flying Rollers had their marginal quarters had all gone out, not until the New and Latter House of Israel was entirely asleep, did he return to his own room and bed, completely exhausted.

But in the morning, when the Pillars met again, Ben Purnell found himself barred from God-House. All of his protests and threats were useless. He could only pace back and forth outside and wait. When he was finally called in, he launched immediately into a new series of mixed and garbled Bible quotations, then announced the revelation that all those who served Mills were unworthy to serve as Pillars, that he was removing them from office and would appoint new Pillars as soon as the Almighty named them for him.

A few of the bearded long-haired men rose and hurried to his side, assuring him that they believed in him. But the majority of them remained seated with Eliza Court.

"We have condemned your blasphemy and heresy," she told him smugly. "The Pillars have ruled that you be banished from the New and Latter House of Israel. All who speak to the heresiarch are defiled and unworthy of the Kingdom."

Ben Purnell shouted her down immediately, thundering that he was excommunicating them, that they had no authority. No one answered except the few who had sided with him. The others filed out of the room one by one, staring right on through him as they passed him, pretending he didn't exist.

Ben wasn't giving up the fight that easily, of course. He went right on campaigning among the Little People. But the Princess and her cronies had spread the word, and the authority of the Prince, his Divine right to rule, had gone unquestioned for so long that the Flying Rollers were thoroughly conditioned to obeying. Only a small minority was willing to speak to Ben that first day and risk eternal damnation. The next day the number was still smaller.

He kept on shouting his claims and his promises at them. He kept on threatening to expose them to the outside world, to give the material from the stolen confessions to the newspapers. But the ostracism closed down tightly and became complete. The Pillars who'd supported him soon repented and begged their Princess for forgiveness. Ben Purnell had to face up to the fact that he was beaten.

Early one morning he loaded his family's few possessions into one of the big pushcarts used by the Israelites in peddling copies of *The Flying Roll*. He piled in as many copies of the book as he could get his hands on, along with the various other religious writings and pamphlets, then, with Mary and little Hettie trudging along behind him, he left the Hamlin Avenue colony and headed south through Detroit.

Nearly penniless, Benjamin Franklin Purnell was just about back where he'd been a dozen years before, when he'd first given up honest bumming to play the part of a preacher. If there was ever a time in his life when he felt like ending the deception, this was it. Full darkness found him in the outskirts of the city. Here he finally shoved the pushcart behind the screen of branches of a roadside thicket, pulled a blanket from the load and spread it.

"Where are we going?" Mary asked him timidly.

"The Lord will guide us," he intoned automatically.

"But what will we do?"

"The Lord will provide. Take no thought for your life, what you shall eat or what you shall drink; nor yet for your body, what you shall put on. Behold the fowls of the air; for they sow not, neither do they reap; yet your heavenly Father feedeth them. Are you not much better than they?"

"But what can we—"

"Oh, shut up and go to sleep!" he snapped at her.

As tired as he was, he lay awake most of the night, puzzling out his future. There seemed to be three choices. He could go on proclaiming himself a prophet and hope to rally the scattered Israelites of other towns behind him. He could rid himself of the eight years' growth of hair and beard and attempt to eke out a living as a way-faring evangelist once again. Or he could give up preaching entirely and look for a regular job. Remembering his days at the broom factory, he ruled out the last alternative immediately.

By morning, he'd made his decision. Pushing on to the next little town, he loaded Mary and Hettie up with copies of *The Flying Roll* and the other sacred writings, then sent them out to peddle this literature from door to door. Next he spent half the day carefully studying a few classic portraits of Christ from some of his pamphlets, then slowly trimming his curly locks and his beard into as close an imitation as possible. He'd managed to hoard away a small amount of money during his years at the New and Latter House of Israel, and he used up almost all of it now to dress himself completely in white—buying a white suit and hat, vest and tie, even white shoes.

He was going to continue playing the part of the Seventh Divine Messenger. He was going to keep on trying to parlay his self-appointed Messiah-hood into the sort of Heaven-on-earth he'd seen Mike Mills so briefly enjoy.

Eight

IN FOSTORIA, Ohio, 1903 is remembered as the year the Fourth of July came in February. An explosion broke out that winter in the big fireworks factory on the edge of town. Everything combustible in the entire plant went up in a prolonged spectacular roar. When the smoke finally cleared, a score of charred bodies lay among the ruins. And one of them was little Hettie Purnell, just 16 years old now.

Her father witnessed that colorful blast, from a window of Fostoria's newly built Israelite church. The explosion came just as a good share of the congregation was filing in for a special service, and Ben Purnell was puzzling over how he'd word a new proposal he had for some parents in his long-haired flock. For a couple of teen-age girls had caught his eye, and he'd decided the time had come to install an institution similar to Mike Mills' ill-fated God-Head here in his newly founded kingdom.

When the first thundering roar split the winter-morning stillness, Ben's train of thought was interrupted and he moved to the window and stared out across the snow-covered fields. A second blast came, still louder, then a series of steady earth-pounding explosions. Then suddenly, as he stared, a skyrocket rose through the smoke and burst high in the air, opening into a cluster of vivid color. Another shot out horizontally, exploding in the snow. Then another. Roman candles arced off in all directions, tracing strange patterns through the smoke. Pinwheels bounced off across the whitened earth. For several minutes the show went on. Then there was only silence and the distant factory was completely hidden by dark smoke.

His forehead wrinkling furiously, Ben turned away from the window and strode back and forth in his office. This freak occurrence might be considered an omen, a flaming portent, and he was trying desperately to figure out a way to work it into the sermon he was about to preach. A good many of his long-haired followers had most certainly witnessed it from the steps of the church they'd built for him. Pacing and frowning, he studied on the problem for a long time, but no good ideas came and he knew his audience was seated and waiting. Finally he decided to stick to the speech he'd originally prepared, stressing some carefully selected passages from old Wroeite sermons.

He checked his appearance carefully, combing his red-gold beard and his long curly hair, straightening his white tie and vest. Then smiling calmly and angelically, he walked in to greet his flock.

Benjamin Franklin Purnell had come a long way in the eight years that had gone by since he'd been banished from the Detroit colony. Trudging slowly back across the Ohio farmlands with his pushcart, he'd visited each of the Israelite families he'd known in the years before he'd joined Mills' kingdom, tirelessly campaigning as the true Seventh Divine Messenger and denouncing Prince Mike as an imposter. And once again, on the road near the Indiana border, Mary Purnell had come up with a revelation of her own. Once again, she'd discovered she was pregnant.

They'd gone on into Richmond, staying with some of the Israelites who'd first taught Ben Purnell the True Faith, but he hadn't returned to the broom factory. A Divine Messenger could hardly be expected to perform manual labor, so Ben had merely kept on with his street preaching. The new baby had been a boy and they'd named him Coy. Ben had decided the Israelites of Richmond were too few and too poverty-stricken to allow him to found his kingdom there, so as soon as Mary had recovered, the Purnells had gone back on the road again. But Ben had demanded and received enough money from the local Flying Rollers to buy a team of horses and a tarpaulin-covered buckboard. The Seventh Divine Messenger had graduated from a pushcart to a covered wagon.

For several years this strange family of four had toured the Indiana, Kentucky and Ohio towns, exactly like an old-fashioned medicine show. And through these years he'd steadily developed his technique as a showman. He'd bought a half dozen white doves and trained them by sprinkling bird seed on his shoulders, even putting seeds in his ears so that the gullible rural crowds would think the birds were giving him Divine messages when they stuck their bills in. From the moment his daughter Hettie's figure had begun rounding, he'd dressed her as briefly as possible to help attract crowds at his camp meetings. Little Coy had learned to sing hymns almost as soon as he'd learned to talk.

They'd worked their way into the hill country, visiting for a time with the Stollards, then with the Purnells, then wandering back to the north again. One day, near Fostoria, Ohio, they'd met a well-to-do Israelite farmer named Ben Pelton.

"I always knew Mike Mills wasn't the real Seventh Messenger," Pelton had told them. "He never fooled me for a moment."

"Many good souls were deceived by the heresiarch,"

Ben Purnell had shaken his head sadly. "How is it you were able to see his falseness so quickly, Brother?"

"He didn't have any message. The first six Messengers all had messages. All of them turned out Sacred Writings. Mills never wrote anything."

The thought had fascinated Ben Purnell. "Strange that you should mention that, Brother Pelton," he'd smiled. "I've been meaning to put the True Gospel into modern print for some time, but moving around the way we've been doing, bringing the True Faith to as many souls as possible, it's been difficult finding the proper calm for meditation and revelation."

Pelton had been impressed. "You folks like to stay on here awhile, I'd be honored."

The Divine Messenger and his family had stayed on for more than a year. And although it was really the first time he'd thought of the idea, Ben Purnell had gone to work on a Sacred Writing. The prose he'd turned out had been a clumsy mixture of Biblical quotations and his own personal interpretation of them, wild allegorical ravings in some places, sheer monotonous repetition in others. But Brother Pelton had been overjoyed, certain he'd aided in the creation of a work every bit as vital as the Bible. He'd put up $1200 to have this masterpiece, which Ben Purnell entitled *The Star of Bethlehem*, published by a printer in Ashland, Ohio.

A neighboring Israelite farm couple, Silas and Cora Mooney, had been privileged to read the new Sacred Writing in manuscript, and they too had been overjoyed, begging the red-bearded prophet to come and be their guest for a while. When several months had passed with no word from the printer, who'd already been paid, Ben Purnell had gone up to Ashland to see what was holding things up. Interestingly enough, he'd taken Cora Mooney, who'd become deeply infatuated with him, along on this trip, leaving Mary and the kids at Fostoria with Silas.

Arriving at Ashland, Ben and Cora had discovered that the printer hadn't as yet even started on *The Star of Bethlehem*. To speed him up, they'd moved into his front office and stayed there, refusing to leave, singing hymns and meeting all arguments with reproachful sermons. The harassed printer had worked his men overtime and run his presses day and night to rush the job through and get rid of them.

As copies of the new Sacred Writing circulated among the Israelites and received an enthusiastic reception, more and more of the long-haired cultists had begun to accept Ben Purnell as the true Seventh Messenger. (After finishing his prison sentence, Mike Mills had fled the country, vowing never to return, taking Eliza Court with him. The Detroit New and Latter House of Israel was rapidly breaking up.) There were quite a few Flying Rollers in the surrounding area and some of them were quite wealthy. Accordingly, Ben had gone into a trance and received the revelation that Fostoria would be a suitable site for the Seventh Kingdom.

Deeply honored, the local cultists had scraped together enough money to build a church for him. In an attempt to wipe out any association with the now-notorious Detroit colony, Ben had given his new kingdom a different name—the House of David. It had been a proud day for him when he'd held his first service there. To honor this occasion, he'd announced, the Holy Ghost would descend at the next service and choose the Virgin of Israel by planting a mystic sign on her forehead.

The new church had been crowded for that second service. Hopeful mothers had brought along their young daughters as potential candidates, freshly scrubbed, dressed in their freshest prettiest white. (Ben's own daughter Hettie hadn't been among them. She'd been sent to work full-time at the nearby fireworks factory when the Purnells had first moved into Fostoria.) But to everyone's surprise, the mystic sign had appeared on the forehead of Cora Mooney. No one had been more surprised than Silas.

"The Lord moves in mysterious ways," Ben Purnell had reminded his flock as Cora beamed happily and the rest scratched their long-haired heads.

In spite of this strange beginning, the Fostoria House of David had prospered and had soon rivaled the former Detroit colony in size. And like Mike Mills before him, Ben had played his Messiah-hood for all it was worth, demanding every cent he could get from the cultists who worshiped him. But just as he'd decided the time was ripe for beginning the religious education of the young girls of the sect, educating them in the manner he'd learned from Prince Mike, that freak explosion had erupted in the distance—like an ancient omen, like a weird colorful portent. He had gone in to preach his sermon inwardly disturbed. It had seemed to him there was something he was overlooking about that strange mid-morning display, something that could cause serious trouble.

The interruption came just as the Israelite service was ending. In spite of Ben's premonition of trouble, the meeting had gone smoothly. Even his revelation about the new institution the Almighty had ordered established in the House of David, an institution he'd named the Inner Mystic Circle to avoid any association with Michael Mills' famed God-Head, had been well received, with the parents of the chosen teen-age girls even smiling proudly at being honored in this way. The congregation was rising to leave when a loud knocking came from the front door of the building. All heads were turned. Impatiently, Ben hurried down the aisle.

"Mr. Purnell?" A uniformed sheriff's deputy stood outside the door, a big man who fidgeted uneasily as he looked in at the beards and the long hair.

"Yes," Ben answered him crisply. "What is it?"

"Well, you probably seen the explosion. There was some people killed and . . . well, your daughter was one of 'em."

Ben Purnell stood perfectly still, his face frozen, trying desperately to think. Watching the blast from the window, he'd been so absorbed in the coming service that he'd forgotten about Hettie entirely. He heard Mary break out crying behind him. Turning, he saw the faces of his followers staring at him in startled disbelief.

All at once he realized what was wrong. He'd promised eternal life to all who believed in him. Whenever a local Israelite had died, Ben had immediately preached a sermon denouncing this person, insisting that the dead cultist had doubted and disobeyed him. Among the many strange rites he'd introduced, there were no funeral services. Now, quite naturally, the House of David congregation was wondering how their Divine Messenger's own daughter could possibly die. Caught in a terrible trap, Ben Purnell turned away quickly, back to face the deputy.

"We need you to claim the body now," the big man explained sympathetically.

His face still expressionless, Ben slowly shook his head.

"Your daughter's body." The deputy was puzzled.

Ben drew a deep breath. "I have no daughter!" he announced, coldly and clearly.

"Your daughter Hettie." The man was startled. "Hettie Purnell."

"I have no daughter," Ben repeated firmly.

"Don't you understand? Your daughter was killed. Now you got to come claim the body—"

On the face of the red-bearded prophet, there was no hint of emotion whatsoever.

"I've told you twice that I have no daughter," he said. "Now this happens to be a place of worship, a church of Christ. And it happens there's a service going on. So if you've nothing further to tell me. . . ."

It took the puzzled deputy several full minutes to finally realize that, for some strange reason connected with this unusual church, its white-suited leader was actually refusing to claim the body of his own daughter. And then the officer's amazement changed to anger.

"You'd better get over there to claim that body and do it quick!" he warned.

After he'd gone, Ben Purnell turned to face his followers.

"She had doubted me," he told them in a pained voice. "She had disobeyed me and mocked the commandments of the Most High that were revealed to me. She doubted me and this was her punishment. As the Written Word

warns, she was cast into a lake of fire. And such will be
the punishment of all those who scorn and mock!"

Using his own daughter's death as a springboard, Benjamin Franklin Purnell launched himself into a second
sermon that day. Far from bringing suspicion and doubt,
the explosion at the fireworks factory served only to
strengthen his hold on the Israelites, for it seemed impossible to the bearded cultists that a mere human being
could receive such news with such matter-of-fact calmness. Obviously, this man was truly a prophet and more,
a Divine Being.

But the rest of the citizens of Fostoria saw things
a little differently. Enraged by what had happened, they
gave the girl a public burial, a funeral as lavish as any the
town had ever known. Every regular church in the area
took up a special collection for flowers. An undertaker
donated his services and an expensive coffin. The crowd
that watched Hettie laid to rest was surprisingly large,
and when the funeral was over little angry groups of
men collected on the streets.

"The Long-Hairs say he's immortal!" men muttered,
again and again. "Putting a rope around his neck would
be one sure way to find out!"

By evening the muttering had become a growling roar,
the sound of a crowd becoming a mob. While the sheriff
hurriedly begged more deputies from neighboring counties, the men of Fostoria laid siege to the House of
David. Crouching fearfully with Mary and young Coy
in a dark corner of a rear room, Ben Purnell heard the
windows of his church being shattered.

He crept to the back door to look for a path of escape,
but there too the mob was waiting. The flickering torches
they carried cast a circle of light entirely around the
house. He was surrounded and trapped, without even a
God to turn to in prayer.

Once again he'd gambled. Once again he'd lost.

Just as the front door was being smashed in, the howl
of the mob was broken by a new sound—the sharp, ringing shouts of organized men efficiently tackling a dangerous assignment. A small band of deputies moved in

boldly, driving back the mob, then beginning the long hard task of dispersing it.

After what seemed like many hours to the Divine Messenger cowering inside, the mob began moving off toward their homes. But the victory of law and order was strictly a temporary one and the sheriff knew this full well.

"You'd do best to get out of town," he suggested to Ben Purnell, after he'd pounded for a long time on the shattered door and the white-clothed Messenger had finally appeared. "The sooner, the better. We might not be able to stop them next time. Don't know as we really want to very much, anyway. A lot of the boys would just as soon join them."

Calling his supporters together first thing in the morning, he announced a new revelation. The Almighty had just informed him that the Lost Tribes of Israel had better migrate in a hurry—to the small lakeside city of Benton Harbor, Michigan.

This came as no particular surprise to any of the Fostoria Israelites, for it was well known that a large number of their brethren, including many of those left leaderless at the Detroit colony when Prince and Princess Michael had fled the country, were now living in the Benton Harbor area. A pair of Flying Roller brothers named Baushke, owners of a prosperous carriage factory there, had been corresponding with Ben Purnell for some time and had accepted him as the true Seventh Messenger. They'd been inviting him to come to Benton Harbor. Now he quickly wired them that he was on his way.

Mary and Coy went with him, of course. So did Cora and Silas Mooney and three more of his most loyal followers. Others from the Fostoria flock assured him of their devotion, gave him as much money as they could scrape together and promised to follow as soon as they could sell their property and get their affairs in order.

Leaving Fostoria was a far cry from the way he'd left Detroit eight years earlier. Instead of stumbling down the road with the pushcart, he was riding first class in a railway coach with faithful cultists eager to wait on him like servants, with money in his pocket, with his future reasonably secure. But even so, Fostoria had still been another failure in his life, and he was 42 years old now. As the train sped north toward Michigan, he meditated carefully, puzzling over all the mistakes he'd made or see made in the decade and a half that had gone by.

From the vantage point of hindsight, Ben Purnell could see that Mike Mills had committed a far more serious error than merely allowing a troublesome jealous wife to stay with him, an error even more fatal than welcoming an ambitious young rival into the fold. Prince Michael had founded his kingdom within the boundaries of a large city, surrounding himself with hostile outsiders. And then in Fostoria, Ben could see now, he'd made exactly the same mistake himself. He'd let his church be located inside an unsympathetic town.

This was the vital lesson that lay in the past. Location was everything. The site of the In-gathering had to be close enough to a city so that the Little People of the sect could find profitable employment, yet still far enough away to provide an essential degree of privacy.

The moment Ben Purnell arrived in Benton Harbor, he acted on this reasoning.

"We certainly hope you enjoy our little city," the two Baushke brothers welcomed him.

Ben surprised them by shaking his head decisively. "It is clear to me already that sinfulness is everywhere here. The unbelieving and the abominable throng the streets. The ungodly flourish on every corner."

"Oh, no!" they protested. "This is a wonderful town."

The Seventh Messenger was firm in his decision. "We must turn to the unfouled earth. We must search the fields and forests and find an untainted spot for the In-gathering."

The very next morning, riding in one of the fine Baushke carriages with a real estate broker beside him and the two brothers still puzzling over what was going on, Ben Purnell toured the outskirts of Benton Harbor. When the carriage drew abreast of a likely looking piece of land just a few miles outside the city, the Seventh Angelic Messenger suddenly pressed the fingers of one hand to his temple.

"That's far enough!" he announced. "This is the right place!"

Returning to Benton Harbor, Ben called an immediate meeting of all the Flying Rollers in the area, sending out word that a very important announcement would be made.

"It has been revealed to me that the Millennium will begin in the Year of Our Lord Nineteen Hundred and Six!" he told the long-haired cultists.

They broke into wild joyful cheering. They'd waited a long time for their reward and the rest of the world's punishment.

"Yes, our time of peace and plenty is very near now," the red-bearded prophet intoned melodically. "But there is a great deal to do and we have only three years to prepare ourselves."

He demanded that the faithful come forth with every cent they could possibly raise, selling everything but the barest necessities, and then turn the money over to him so he could buy that tract of land and prepare a suitable place of worship for the final hour.

This demand met surprisingly little resistance. The Israelites were too busy anticipating the pleasure of watching the rest of humanity perish to worry about the fact that they were handing over nearly all they possessed to a stranger. The Baushke brothers came up with an even hundred thousand. Several other large donations followed, with a steady stream of smaller ones.

When the purchase of the land had been completed and construction had been started on two large buildings there, Ben announced that he would personally make a missionary trip to Australia in order to give the surviving members of the Jezreel church, the Sixth Kingdom, a chance to hurry to the In-gathering before the books were sealed. He also arranged for a number of his followers to tour Canada and England to preach the same message.

Then, Benjamin Franklin Purnell—bigamist, hobo, street preacher, broom-maker, pushcart evangelist, the Seventh Messenger, Shiloh, younger brother of Christ and leader of the Lost Tribes of Israel—added a new title to his collection. He had himself officially proclaimed King Benjamin, King of the Seventh Kingdom, King of the Israelite House of David, Church of the New Eve, Body of Christ.

And King Benjamin he would remain, for twenty-three full years.

Nine

ON MARCH 27, 1905, curious crowds gathered to watch as a long procession moved up Water Street and trudged on through Benton Harbor, on toward the grounds of the new Israelite colony. Eighty-five men, women and children, carrying all their worldly goods in cheap canvas duffel sacks, marched by. The House of David's Australian immigrants had arrived.

King Ben's whirlwind tour of Australia had been a stormy one. Feeling against the "Beardies" had been strong in many towns, and the fear that this redheaded evangelist from the States would bring back the days of Wroe and Jezreel had precipitated a number of violent riots. But once the citizens had realized that Ben Purnell was urging the Israelites to migrate to America, he'd received full co-operation from everyone.

Mary had accompanied him. So had Cora Mooney and several of the choicest teen-age daughters of Benton Harbor Israelites. After firmly instructing the converts he'd won to ship out steerage in order to save money, the king himself had returned first-class with his attendants. It had been a pleasant relaxing cruise after his strenuous preaching campaign. And he'd returned home to the pleasant news that the missionaries he'd sent out through England and Canada had done remarkably well. In less than two years, the population of Ben Purnell's kingdom had grown to nearly 500.

Now, from the window of his royal quarters on the second floor of the fine new building he'd named Shiloh, the red-bearded monarch watched his converts arrive. He estimated their number and worth very quickly, singling out and appraising the young women among them and the girls who would soon be young women. Turning away from the window, he checked his appearance carefully before a large ornate mirror and sprinkled a few grains of bird seed on his shoulders. The shrewd and calculating look on his face dissolved and was replaced by a glow of Divine piety. Then he started down to officially welcome the Australian newcomers.

He moved down the long line of converts, shaking hands, greeting them one by one.

"I'm Isabelle Pritchard," a woman with two little girls, scarcely more than babies, told him. "I don't know if you remember me. You talked to my husband mostly. He's dead now, but we came, anyway. This is Irene and this is Hilda."

Although his face hid it, Ben winced inside. He wanted able-bodied productive men in his kingdom, not costly dependants.

"That's most unfortunate," he nodded sympathetically. "If only he could have held on to life long enough to join the In-gathering! In the True Faith death is, of course, unknown."

One of the two little girls spoke up. "We don't have any papa any more," she told him shyly.

He knelt down and patted both their heads. "Don't you worry," he assured them. "I'll be your papa from now on."

Their mother looked about her, a happy smile on her face. The grounds were green and well kept, shaded by great trees. Over near the arch that joined Shiloh with the new building being constructed beside it, a small band of long-haired, bearded musicians were softly playing hymn music "It's so peaceful here—a real refuge from the whole world!"

Ben Purnell nodded. "Would you like to turn in now?" he asked matter-of-factly.

"That would be nice," the widow answered. "It was a rough trip with these two to handle."

Ben shook his head, smiling patiently. "You don't understand. Would you like to turn in now? Lay not up for yourself treasures upon earth, for where your treasure is, there will your heart be also."

Mrs. Pritchard still didn't follow him.

"If you will be perfect," he lectured her, a little more firmly now, "go and sell that which you have, and give to the poor, and you shall have treasure in heaven. Do little children hoard earthly wealth?"

"Oh!" the widow exclaimed. "You mean the money!"

Ben Purnell nodded. "If you're ready to turn in now, the young lady in the office there will help you." He pointed at the first floor of Shiloh.

"There's only about seventeen hundred left," Mrs. Pritchard told him. "Time we paid for the funeral and got our passage—"

"The amount is unimportant," King Ben lied. "All that really matters is that you hold nothing back upon entering the kingdom."

Again and again, all down the long line of immigrants, this little scene was repeated.

Benjamin Franklin Purnell, throughout the last few years, had been formulating a few unusual personal theories about the best way to rule a religious cult. Now, without hesitating, he was testing his theories.

Ben had never studied psychology, or much of anything else, but he'd shrewdly guessed that all cultists and extreme fanatics have a strong inner desire, even an actual need, for suffering. He'd decided to operate on the principle that his Israelites were basically little different from the Penitentes or the Holy Men of the Far East, who prove their faith by whipping themselves, sleeping on beds of spikes or mutilating their bodies.

If what the Flying Rollers really wanted was suffering, King Ben figured, he was just the man to give it to them.

Shiloh was completed now, and another large ornate building, to be named Jerusalem, was nearly finished beside it. And yet both were strictly reserved for Ben's own lavish apartment, for his business offices, for the smaller apartments of his chief Pillars, and for the quarters of the young girls who were currently undergoing blood-purification rites. For the Little People of the sect, crude tiny log cottages were built in the woods across the road, containing only the simplest and cheapest of furnishings.

"These things are deeply symbolic," he patiently explained to those who questioned this vast difference in standards of living. "Everything your Messenger does he does only to test you, you must remember, to test your fitness to enter the Kingdom."

As Mike Mills had done before him, Ben Purnell granted his followers only the plainest articles of clothing once he'd relieved them of the burden of all their possessions. Also like Mills, he demanded that they give up liquor, tobacco and meat. And if an occasional Israelite girl who'd been sent to live at Shiloh set free whispers about the steak dinners, the cigarettes or the beer and wine parties that were routine in the royal quarters, the King's explanation was always the same—he was merely testing their faith in him.

Remembering how Prince Mike's attorney had almost saved him with the use of Bernice Bickle's confession, Ben Purnell demanded that all who entered the Seventh Kingdom write out full and detailed lifetime confessions. If one of these was found to contain nothing that might later be used against its author, King Ben would tear it up and demand another, angrily insisting that only by revealing all sins, and confessing and repenting, could anyone hope for eternal life. Many misguided souls actually invented crimes to satisfy the Divine Messenger.

After a lifetime confession had finally been accepted, monthly confessions were required. Since there was little opportunity for sinning in the House of David, most of these were dull and worthless, but Ben had a number of trusted assistants known as "Sweepers" who read all confessions, filed important bits of information for him and burned the rest.

Drunk with power now, Ben began switching the Little People from one crude shack to another at least once a week to keep them from ever feeling the slightest trace of ownership. He went further and ordered all his subjects to abstain from normal marital relations, imposing what he called the Virgin Law. Even kissing was outlawed. He justified this from the Bible, Revelations 14:4 —"These are they which were not defiled with women; for they are Virgins. . . . These were redeemed from among men." But the simple truth was that King Ben was unsatisfied merely to have free choice of practically all women in his kingdom; he'd decided he wanted to have them exclusively.

Benjamin Franklin Purnell discovered he'd guessed correctly. His cultists loved punishment. The more wretched they were as a result of his treatment and the greater the contrast between the life he led and the life he prescribed for them, the more invincible his rule became.

A few members of the Israelite colony, of course, objected to some of his most extreme measures. If all of Ben's eloquent alternating promises and threats failed to silence a rebellious Flying Roller's protests, a brief conference with the man would be held behind closed doors at Shiloh. Then, for the first time, the disillusioned cultist would see his king as he really was—not a prophet but a shrewd ruthless con-man.

"Here's a ten-dollar bill and a railroad ticket to Chicago," he'd announce, crisp and businesslike. "Good-bye, Brother."

"What about the money I turned in when I came here?" the apostate Israelite would demand.

Ben would laugh. "You're a better man rid of it, Brother. It's easier for a camel to pass through the eye of a needle than for a rich man to enter the Kingdom of Heaven."

"I want that money back!"

"See a lawyer then. You'll be told you have no right to demand the return of gifts made to this church or any other."

"All right!" the man might threaten. "I'm going straight to the nearest newspaper office and see what they think about all this. I'll let the whole world know what goes on here."

King Ben would shake his head, open the man's file and read aloud a few choice paragraphs from his confessions.

"In that case," he'd explain, "I'd also have to let the world know just what kind of a man was making these charges, wouldn't I? No, Brother. You'd do best to take that train to Chicago and just forget our little community even exists!"

In his dealings with the various businessmen of Benton Harbor, Ben Purnell also proved extremely down to earth for a prophet. When the local price of lumber seemed too high, he leased a timber-cutting site farther north on the lake shore and sent a crew of bearded Israelites up to cut the wood he needed for colony buildings. Then he bought a lake schooner, the *Rising Sun*, and used it to bring the lumber back, both for the House of David buildings and to sell on the open market.

In some ways, these first years at Benton Harbor, King Ben was still the medicine-show pitchman he'd been in his covered-wagon days. He sent a large colorful House of David exhibition to the St. Louis World's Fair, complete with music and attractive young Israelite girls to preach the True Faith and peddle copies of *The Star of Bethlehem*. He began making plans for an even more spectacular display at the coming Chicago World's Fair. But it was mainly in his regular preaching to his flock that his talent for show business came out.

There are many men living today who heard Ben Purnell preach—a never-to-be-forgotten experience, for his sermons were as colorful as his red-gold hair and beard. He would launch into terrifying descriptions of the torture that awaited the unfaithful—the seven great plagues, the bottomless pit, the lake of burning brimstone. Roaring like a bull elk or sobbing like a lost bear cub in the night, he'd paint such detailed and graphic pictures of eternal damnation that few Flying Rollers could doubt their king's claim that he had actually seen these things.

Abruptly, his voice would grow calm and smooth and hypnotic as he described just as eloquently the golden city with the jewel-studded foundations and the twelve gates of pearl—the reward for the faithful as soon as the Millennium arrived.

Finally, when his flock was as charged up emotionally as he could get them, he'd begin shouting questions at them, bringing them to their feet as they answered. Did they believe in him? Would they cast off all earthly values and accept his Message? Did they trust him? Would they receive the True Faith as he revealed it? Would they follow him into the golden city?

Strangely enough, the Tabernacle where these services were held, directly across the street from Shiloh and Jerusalem, was a plain inexpensive structure, very much like a public meeting hall. It was very much as though King Ben was so sure of his hold on his followers, so certain of their trust, that he was openly mocking them by providing the simplest, cheapest place of worship possible and placing it close to his own luxurious quarters.

The most crucial test of his power, through all those early years, came in the late months of 1906, when the Israelites were breathlessly waiting, day by day, for the Millennium he'd promised. But King Ben met this problem head on and proved equal to it. Calling a gigantic mass meeting of all his subjects, he spent two full hours lecturing and upbraiding them severely for their sinfulness, for their evil thoughts, for their lack of faith in him. And when he had them fully convinced of their unworthiness, he announced a startling new revelation. The Almighty was so angered by their lack of devotion to His prophet that He'd postponed the Millennium, putting it off until some indefinite date in the future.

It worked. There were a few Flying Rollers who felt

they'd been tricked and began planning to leave. But the very great majority of the Israelites filed out of the Tabernacle that day searching their consciences for the slightest taint of doubt or disobedience, determining to prove their faith and devotion to their Divine Messenger in every way possible.

Benjamin Franklin Purnell would give them plenty of chances to prove their faith. For from the very beginning, he'd been carrying on the old Wroeite practices of blood-cleansing or female circumcision. He'd established the Inner Mystic Circle he'd been planning at Fostoria, keeping anywhere from 15 to 20 teen-age girls quartered in a series of small rooms that adjoined his royal apartment, discarding the older ones when he tired of them, bringing in new ones as soon as they blossomed and caught his eye. There, behind the drawn shades of Shiloh, King Ben was gluttonizing himself on a scale that made Prince Mike's former God-Head seem almost like monogamy.

Ten

OF THE DOZENS of Israelite daughters with whom the red-bearded prophet amused himself throughout the early years of his reign, two girls—Esther Johnson and Hazel Ruth Wade—eventually played the most important roles in the explosive climax of his fantastic career. Strangely enough, neither of the two was ever actually a harem favorite. Esther was a shrewd, highly capable, highly trusted assistant and personal secretary who went on to play the part of a House of David hatchet girl in many of Ben Purnell's later times of trouble. Hazel Ruth was a superbly skilled evangelist, capable of breaking a potential convert's heart with her beautiful hymn-singing voice and her convincing soft-throated preaching. Benjamin Franklin Purnell saw immediately that both could be extremely valuable to him. He would learn later that both could be dangerous.

Esther Johnson was a pretty little Swedish girl, slim and pert and quick-witted. Her father was a California tailor who brought his son and four daughters to the colony the first year of its existence, leaving his invalid wife behind, intending to send for her the moment he was settled. He dutifully turned in all his money, and Esther's mother remained in California until her death. King Ben had little use for invalids in his kingdom.

The bearded king noticed Esther immediately, noticed her quick-to-learn mind and her crisp speaking voice. All of the colony children were lectured regularly on the Sacred Writings, including Ben's own. It was, in fact, the only schooling they received. But for the Johnson girl, King Ben ordered a great deal of special tutoring, an extensive course on every phase of Israelite doctrine. In 1904, when she was only 14, she was already doing missionary work, touring the country in one of the many House of David covered wagons along with three older Flying Roller preachers. At this point she firmly believed Ben Purnell was a Divine being. It was the following year that he disillusioned her.

They were aboard the House of David schooner *Rising Sun* at the time. It was Ben's habit, in pleasant weather, to ride his ship up to his timber-cutting tract and then to picnic on the beach while the boat was being loaded, invariably with a dozen or so teen-age girls for company. Just back from a missionary tour, 15-year-old Esther was delighted when she was invited along on one of these outings. But on the return trip, as the king sun-bathed on a couch on deck, two of his favorites whispered something in his ear and pointed to Esther. He called her over.

"The other girls think it's about time you were initiated into the Inner Mystic Circle," he told her, laughing. There had been wine along on that picnic, Esther had been shocked to learn. Ben had gulped down a great deal himself and even given it to several of the girls.

"Into what?"

"They think it's time your blood was purified."

"How?" she asked cautiously. The girls clustered around the king's couch were giggling steadily.

"Well," he smiled at her, "you might start by taking your clothes off."

She stared at him in startled disbelief, then glanced about her. They were on the roof deck, out of sight of the long-haired crew members or the Israelite men returning from work assignments in the lumber camp.

"Here?"

"Why not? Are you afraid to undress in front of the other girls, Esther?"

"Well, no, but—"

"Oh, I see!" He scowled suddenly. "Then it's me!" His voice was low and ominous. "Tell me, Esther. Do you think of me as a mere mortal man?"

"No!" she said quickly. "Of course not. Of course, I don't." Doubting Ben's divinity was the most serious crime an Israelite could commit.

"Do you understand the True Faith, Esther?"

"I think I do."

"Are you willing to be tried—to sacrifice everything for the Faith?"

"I think I am."

"Do you know how to attain immortality?"

"By living in the True Faith and adhering to its commandments."

"That isn't always enough, Esther. You see, you lived in the outside world for many years before you came here. Evil is everywhere there and you could not help but have your blood tainted. Then, too, you go into the outside world again and again in search of converts, talking to unbelievers regularly. This is why your blood must be cleansed. My blood is different from the blood of mortal men. My blood is absolutely pure. Only by sowing the seeds of purity in your body and making your blood pure can I be sure of giving you immortality."

The young girl stood there silent and confused.

"Now take off your clothes, Esther." His voice was still kindly, but a note of firmness had come into it, as though he'd been patient enough in his explanation and wanted his commands obeyed instantly now.

Sudden revulsion welled up inside Esther Johnson. "No!" she gasped, terrified at the very thought of disobeying the Divine Messenger.

With the cluster of harem girls watching him closely to see how he'd answer such outrageous disobedience, Ben Purnell didn't hesitate. In sudden anger, he jumped up from the couch, grabbed Esther, carried her to the rail and held her over the side, high above the deep dark water of Lake Michigan which moved swiftly past below. He held her there for a full half-minute, while she screamed and begged for her life. Then he carried her back and tossed her roughly on that couch.

"Now you have just one more chance to do as you're told!" he threatened her.

Sick with fear, sobbing steadily, she disrobed completely and was forced to submit to him with all the other girls looking on.

As a member of the Inner Circle, Esther was ordered to leave the shack where her father and brother and sisters were quartered and to move into one of the small rooms that sided Ben's royal apartment on the second floor of Shiloh. As she gradually became accustomed to the life that was prescribed for her, King Ben put her to work in the business office downstairs. Since the great majority of the Israelites were very simple-minded people, there were few Ben could trust with important assignments. More and more, he came to depend on the young Johnson girl. Just a few months after he'd first seduced her, he sent her to England on a highly delicate mission.

"First thing after you get off the boat," he ordered her, "you go see this Lizzie Tomlinson. She must turn to the True Faith and join the In-gathering. This is very important."

"Why is any one soul so important?" she asked, trying to rationalize reality with the theories of the Sacred Writings.

King Ben stared at her a moment, then decided to be frank with her.

"This one soul's worth about twenty thousand dollars, and we could use it. Carrying on the Lord's work can be expensive, you know."

"Oh."

"When you've got the Tomlinson woman converted," he went on," you're to call on this Mr. Corey. He's in charge of what's left of the Fifth Kingdom and whatever money and property the English branch of the old Wroeite church has left. I want you to convince him it's his duty to turn everything in to the Seventh Kingdom."

"How?" Esther asked.

"How!" He stared at her a moment, then laughed softly. "Purify his blood for him. You have to be ready to sacrifice anything for the True Faith. Don't worry— I'll absolve you of any sin."

The girl blushed. "Suppose he's too old to be affected that way?"

"Too old!" King Ben snorted. "No man's too old. If I ever get too old, you can personally give me a drug and put me out of my misery. Now get going or you'll miss your boat. And don't let your missionary zeal run away with you and convert a bunch of paupers to bring back here. The Seventh Kingdom simply cannot endure against the evil in the world if it weakens itself by trying to support half of the riffraff of the world."

Ben Purnell eventually had to go into the English courts to get the remaining Fifth Church funds from Mr. Corey, but the Johnson girl did succeed in bringing back the Tomlinson woman and the $20,000. And as the years went by, Esther became more and more of a Girl Friday to her king in running the intricate affairs of the House of David, always in the sincere belief, ingrained from childhood, that the various despicable things she was forced to do would benefit the True Faith and the Seventh Kingdom in the end. She arranged secret burials for those who died from sickness after Ben Purnell refused to waste money on doctors. She talked rebellious young harem-members who were trying to flee the colony into first signing statements testifying to the purity of conduct of their king. She even obtained such a statement from her own sister Lena. On one typical assignment, she arranged a compromising situation for a girl Ben Purnell feared would talk, luring her into a hotel room, trapping her there with a married Israelite man and hiring photographers to record the manufactured indiscretion. Once she even turned her appealing young charms on a governor of Michigan in an attempt to talk him out of a threatened state investigation of the House of David.

In carrying out her duties as a confidential secretary, she was skilled and deadly. But a time would come when King Ben would foolishly turn her against him. And as an enemy, she would prove just as deadly.

Hazel Ruth Wade was two years younger than Esther Johnson. Her father, Richard T. Wade, had once been the sheriff of Wichita County, Kansas, but he'd settled down on an Oklahoma farm after marrying a girl named Leonora, an extremely religious girl so opposed to violence that she'd ordered him to lay aside his sixguns and to give up his career as a law enforcer if he wanted her for a wife. Years later, on a pleasure trip to the St. Louis World's Fair, she's seen the House of David sideshow, taken the literature home to study, then written in asking for more information. King Ben had sent August Baushke to convert the family.

"What are you planting apple trees for?" Baushke scoffed at their farm. "The end of the world's coming in just two years! You'll never pick those apples, Brother. You'd best hurry to the In-gathering of Israel and save yourself and your family."

Both the former sheriff and his oldest daughter Edna were cautious and suspicious. But Leonora Wade embraced the Israelite faith instantly and wholeheartedly. With her three other daughters, Hazel Ruth, Cleatus and

Dorothy, and her son Hayden, she followed the bearded missionary back to the Benton Harbor colony in 1904.

"I remember when I first saw the House of David," Hazel Ruth, 12 years old at the time, wrote years later. "We came past Jerusalem and past the arch and the lawns were green and beautiful. The band was lined up out in front, playing. Queen Mary was waiting on the steps of Shiloh to greet us. Then King Benjamin came out and stood beside her. He was all dressed in white and doves were swarming about his head and lighting on his shoulders. Why, I thought I was going right into the gates of Paradise!"

Her father and her older sister Edna followed, to try to talk her mother into returning. Ben Purnell went to work on the former sheriff and almost persuaded him to join the colony. Richard Wade even sold his farm and brought the money to Benton Harbor. It was in talking finances that King Ben lost this convert.

"My girl Edna ain't going to join no matter what anyone says to her," Wade informed the long-haired prophet. "We got fourteen thousand dollars, altogether. What do you figure I ought to give Edna?"

"Why give her anything?" Ben asked.

"Well, you know." Richard Wade shrugged. "A man always tries to leave his kids something."

"You mean when he dies?"

"Yeah."

"Well, if you live in the True Faith, Brother, you're never going to die. So why give the girl anything?"

This greediness on the part of a supposed Divine being made the former sheriff suspicious again and he decided against entering the colony. He rented a house in downtown Benton Harbor instead and lived there with his daughter Edna. When his wife demanded half of their money, he gave it to her, even though he knew it would be promptly turned in to King Ben. Then for five long years he stayed on in the city, trying to get Leonora to come back to him. Finally, in 1909, he gave up and left the state.

In the meantime, at the age of 14, Hazel Ruth was

initiated into Ben Purnell's Inner Mystic Circle. She left
the crude shack assigned to her family and moved into
one of the many little rooms that completely surrounded
the royal Shiloh apartment. On the first night King Ben
came in to sit on the edge of her bed.

"Do you like it here, Ruth?"

"Yes." She was shaking with nervousness at being so
close to a Divine being.

"Are you studying the True Faith?"

She nodded. She'd been attending the only school in
the colony, the class held in the Tabernacle across the
street in which the Sacred Writings were read aloud to
the children.

"Have you been told anything at all about blood purification?" he asked softly.

When she shook her head, he began explaining clearly
and concisely all of the theory behind the old Wroeite
doctrines. But when he attempted to put the theory into
practice and began pulling off her nightgown, she broke
out crying and kicked and shoved him away.

He left her alone for the rest of that night, but he
locked the door as he went out. The next morning, however, Hazel Ruth managed to slip out of Shiloh and to
run back through the woods to her mother's little cottage. Choking and breathing hard, she told what had
happened.

"You'll burn in Hell if you talk that way!" Leonora
Wade warned her daughter, sending the other children
out of hearing. "Don't you realize King Benjamin is not
a mortal man? How could he possibly do anything like
that? You must have just had a nightmare. Now enough
of this! I'm taking you back to Shiloh and you pay attention to what King Benjamin says and behave yourself. Otherwise, you'll burn in Hell, I'm warning you!"

Forcibly returned to the harem-quarters by her own
mother, Hazel Ruth still remained stubborn. King Ben
merely let the environment work on her for a while, giving her a reasonable chance to realize that all the girls
were doing it. He put an older harem girl in with her
as a roommate. He even cleansed the blood of other girls

in her presence. But when several weeks had gone by
and she still remained unclaimed, he came into her room
one evening, ordered her roommate out, then tore off
her clothing in grim silence, slapping her soundly and
repeatedly until she submitted to his sexual invasion of
her virginal body.

As was often the case with newcomers, Hazel Ruth
was the red-bearded prophet's favorite for some time,
and he treated her very much as a child treats a new toy.
He often talked baby talk to her. Each evening he
would sit her on his knee and have her read his newspaper to him. Eventually he grew tired of her and became absorbed in other new additions to the Inner Mystic Circle, among them her kid-sister, Cleatus. It was
then that he sent Hazel Ruth out on her first missionary
tour.

Since jobs for teen-age girls were extremely scarce
in that era, this was the most profitable use King Ben
could make of them, at the same time relieving able-
bodied men from preaching duty so they could work at
full-time jobs to enrich their king. Most of the young
girls were hopelessly poor evangelists and served only
to attract a crowd to the camp meetings held beside the
covered wagons, so that Israelite elders could do the real
preaching. But young Hazel Ruth developed a knack for
this sort of work.

Like Esther Johnson, Hazel Ruth Wade was small and
pretty. Otherwise they were opposites in every way.
Where Esther was sharp-featured and sharp-tongued,
Hazel Ruth was soft-voiced and round-faced, her beauty
childlike and dimpled. Her most striking gift was her
singing voice—rich and husky, appealing and sincere.
She learned to do as much with a hymn as torch singers
do with blues songs. In addition, her preaching was fresh
and sparkling, and she became the House of David's star
performer in the field, attracting converts like flies. On
tour, she was billed as "Salvation Nell."

Returning to Benton Harbor after each period of
proselytizing, she would be given a room at Shiloh and
her king would promptly see that her blood was re-

cleansed of any taint she might have picked up on the road. Then, following a short stretch of harem duty, she'd be sent out on tour in the covered wagon again. For four full years this was the life she led.

Her mother, Leonora Wade, still living in that crude shack with the two youngest children, came down with pneumonia in 1910 and grew steadily worse. Her older sister Edna, married now but still living in Benton Harbor, learned about this and wrote to her father who was working on a farm in Indiana.

Rushing to his wife's side, Richard Wade found her lying unattended with just one thin blanket over her. He found the small drafty cottage heated only by a little wood-burning cookstove, its temperature scarcely above freezing. But Leonora was undisturbed.

"Don't worry, dear," she smiled happily. "I've been keeping the True Faith. I've believed in King Benjamin and done everything he said. How could I possibly die? It's you we must think of, dear. Please, now, join the In-gathering before it's too late."

The former sheriff of Wichita hurried out to bring back warm bedding and a new stove. He called a doctor in and stayed with his wife day and night, fighting for her life. But it was much too late. Weakened by the cheap Israelite diet, chilled incessantly through the long Michigan winter, Leonora lived just five days longer.

Richard Wade turned silently away from her body and strode directly through the snow-fogged woods and across the road to the main office at Shiloh—a tall thin man who still wore a wide-brimmed Western hat. With his face expressionless and his voice soft and low, he asked to see Ben Purnell. But there was something frightening about his apparent lack of emotion, and Executive Secretary Francis Thorpe called Esther Johnson.

"Better get Salvation Nell down here!" he whispered. "He's asking for Benjamin!"

King Ben's Girl Friday hurried up to the second floor, coached Hazel Ruth Wade carefully, urged her to talk her father out of causing any trouble and then sent her down.

"King Benjamin isn't even in the colony right now," Hazel Ruth insisted. "Besides, you can't possibly blame him for what's happened! If Mother had really lived in the True Faith, if she'd honestly believed in him like she said she did, nothing could have—"

"You listen a minute, girl!" the former sheriff interrupted her. "I'm takin' Hayden and Dorothy out of here right now. That's all the room I got in the buggy, but I'll be back after you and Cleatus tomorrow. And you be ready!"

"I can't leave the House of David!" Hazel Ruth was terrified at the thought. "Don't you realize what's coming, Father? Why . . . once the Millennium begins and the books are sealed, this will be the only safe refuge on the face of the earth. I'll show you in the Bible."

"Never mind." Her father shook his head slowly. "You be ready tomorrow. You see that Cleatus is ready, too. And Hazel Ruth!" He waved his hand contemptuously at several bearded men who stared cautiously at him from the far side of the office. "You do these long-hair fellas a favor and tell 'em to keep out of my way, huh?"

His face still looked vacant and expressionless as he left. But once the initial shock of his wife's death wore off, rage ran deep and feverish in Richard Wade. He left his two youngest children with his daughter Edna, went home to Indiana, strapped on beneath his coat the twin revolvers he'd saved but hadn't worn since his days in Wichita, then came back looking for Ben Purnell.

Meanwhile, the moment he'd left the colony, his daughter Hazel Ruth had been rushed to a meeting at which Queen Mary and Cora Mooney were presiding. Some 20 other harem girls were there, but the king himself was not to be seen. The two women explained that there might be trouble, that if the authorities were called in the girls might even be subjected to medical examinations. For this reason, it was bluntly announced, King Benjamin was ordering them all to get married. Having taken this precaution, if examinations were made he could simply blame their husbands. The girls were ordered to choose the names of Israelite boys and to write them down, also listing second choices.

"I don't know any boys," Hazel Ruth Wade complained. Because of her missionary tours and stays in the harem quarters of Shiloh, she'd had little contact with the rest of the colony.

"Surely you remember the names of some boys from school," Cora Mooney, now the official High Priestess of Shiloh, urged her.

The girl thought back a full six years. "Well . . . there was a boy named Ray Hornbeck who sat next to me."

Mary Purnell, standing nearby, shook her head. "Ray Hornbeck has already been chosen."

"Come now, child!" Cora Mooney prodded her impatiently. "You must remember some others. Benjamin has ordered that you be married. If you can't think of anyone, we'll choose someone for you ourselves."

The 18-year-old girl shook her head. "I can remember the names Irving Smith and William Frye. But I can't even remember what they looked like."

"All right." Cora Mooney called another older Flying Roller woman. "Check those two. See if either of them's willing to marry little Salvation Nell here. If not, tell one of them it's a direct commandment from Benjamin and see that you have him at the justice's office in a half-hour."

Not until Hazel Ruth Wade stood before the justice of the peace, who was giving the Israelites a special rate of 50¢ a couple for these mass-production marriages, did she learn who her husband would be. As it turned out she got Irving Smith. Cora Mooney took the newlyweds aside while other couples were being rapidly united.

"Benjamin wants you to escort Salvation Nell on her next missionary tour," she told the perplexed boy. "You're to leave today, immediately. And remember now, you two—this is a marriage in name only. You're both to observe the Virgin Law strictly or you'll suffer the consequences. You understand that these are **Benjamin's** personal commandments?"

Seven other pairs were united in meaningless marriages

that day and 13 the next. At the same time, Esther Johnson was rushing Cleatus Wade and several other Inner Mystic Circle members who were still under the legal marriageable age out of town, registering them under fictitious names in a large Chicago hotel. King Ben had ordered her to keep them out of sight until further notice.

When former-sheriff Wade arrived back at the House of David, determined to test the long-haired prophet's claimed immortality with a .45 slug, Cora Mooney waved a certificate of marriage in his face.

"She's Hazel Smith now," Ben's loyal High Priestess announced curtly. "You have no further claim on her."

Richard Wade studied the document in silence, then crumpled it up and dropped it on the floor of the Shiloh office.

"You get my girl, Cleatus out here right quick!" he ordered softly. "And I want to see Ben Purnell, too."

"Cleatus is off in the East doing missionary work," Cora Mooney insisted. "And Benjamin isn't even in the country right now. He's . . . uh . . . sailing for England on a new preaching tour."

The former sheriff stared at her a moment, then shrugged. "Reckon I'll see for myself." He pushed on past her and started for the stairs.

A long-haired Pillar tried to block his way. Wade caught the man's coat front and beard in both hands, lifted him completely off his feet and tossed him back to crash sprawling across one of the desks. Then he went on up to search the second floor, ignoring the angry shouts below and the shrieks of the girls whose bedrooms he invaded. But he found the royal apartment deserted. And, although most of the newly married Inner Circle members had been promptly returned to the royal harem quarters, neither Cleatus nor Hazel Ruth was among them.

"Where're the Wade girls!" he demanded, again and again. But the frightened young ladies of Shiloh merely cowered in the corners and shook their heads.

His rage beginning to show in his face, he stalked back down the stairs and through the office.

"You'd better get out of here quick!" Cora Mooney snapped at him as he went past her, slamming out the front door and hurrying past the arch toward Jerusalem.

A dozen or more young Flying Roller men were waiting for him on the lawn, heavy clubs in their hands. Richard Wade stopped, unbuttoned and pushed back his coat, then kept on going. The group broke apart, watched him in silence as he kicked open the door of Jerusalem.

Inside, two more of the king's lieutenants blocked his way, one of them even nervously pointing a small pocket revolver at him. His coattails still pushed back, the former sheriff bore down on them.

"You got about two seconds to either go ahead and try somethin' or else step outa the way!" he warned.

They moved aside and he strode through the building on another room-to-room search, probing every corner and closet of the Pillars' apartments, ignoring their indignant protests. But his daughters were not there. And neither was the bearded king.

"He's somewhere here, all right!" he shouted at Queen Mary. "I'll find him no matter how long it takes!" But she merely stared through him in haughty frozen-faced silence.

Out across the street and through the woods he went, pounding on the doors of the Israelite shacks, forcing his way into each of them, his face so dark with anger now that no one tried to stop him. He searched the colony again and again, hour after hour. He threatened the bearded Pillars vehemently, shoved and slapped them around, trying desperately to give his rage an outlet by provoking a fight. But it was all useless. The entire House of David resisted him in passive silence. And there was no sign of his daughters—no sign of Ben Purnell.

He was back the next day and the day after that. He stayed on in Benton Harbor for weeks, storming into the colony at irregular hours, sometimes in the middle of the night, hoping for a glimpse of his girls or an opportunity to take a shot at the long-haired monarch. He finally went to the local authorities, only to find them strongly reluctant to interfere in internal Israelite affairs.

"If your girl Cleatus prefers to live with her married sister, there's nothing much we can do about it," he was told. "I don't know what you expect, when you haven't seen her in years. The people out there say they're off together doing missionary work and that they've already told you they don't want to leave the colony. So your wife died of pneumonia there! That's too bad, but people die of pneumonia everywhere. You've just got to realize that these people have the same right to practise their own religion as anyone else."

Richard T. Wade, the former gun-slinging sheriff of Wichita who'd faced down and bested innumerable varieties of badmen in his day, finally admitted to himself that he was beaten, beaten by a strange brand of outlaw who couldn't be forced to fight. A short time later he returned to Indiana, taking Dorothy and Hayden with him, making a new home for them there.

Not until 17 years later, sitting in a courtroom, testifying and hearing the testimony of others, would be learn where Ben Purnell had been hiding all this time—in the big House of David sideshow tent at the Chicago World's Fair!

Esther Johnson and Hazel Ruth Wade were just two of the dozens and eventually hundreds who served time in the second-floor rooms of Shiloh. The stories later told in court by the long-haired prophet's Girl Friday and his star evangelist, Salvation Nell, were just two single threads in the many-storied fabric of his life and reign. But if Benjamin Franklin Purnell had really been the prophet he claimed to be, if he'd actually been able to foretell the future, he'd have gone ahead and tossed Esther overboard that day on the *Rising Sun* and he'd have left Hazel Ruth with her mother in that colony shack. For these two young ladies were destined to give King Ben more trouble than all of the rest of the girls he debauched combined.

Eleven

THE FACT that the former sheriff of Wichita was gunning for him wasn't the only threat that sent Ben Purnell ducking for cover in that year of 1910. Mrs. Lulu Baushke, the wife of one of the two brothers who'd originally invited the king to Benton Harbor, had decided that Ben's way of repaying her husband's hospitality, by seducing their daughter Harriet, was a little too much to stomach, even for the promise of everlasting life. She'd quarreled violently with her husband and renounced the True Faith, stamping out of the colony in a deadly rage. Now word suddenly reached the bearded monarch that she was coming back after her daughter.

Harriet was a harem favorite, and Ben wasn't willing to give her up. He had Esther Johnson arrange another quick meaningless marriage, then show the certificate to the angry woman when she showed up at the House of David, telling her she had no further claim on the girl. But this didn't satisfy Mrs. Baushke. She brought morals charges against Ben in open court and a warrant was issued for his arrest. The Seventh Divine Messenger fled to Canada and went into hiding there.

Such skilled lieutenants as Esther Johnson, Cora Mooney and Queen Mary were eventually able to silence the threat. From Harriet's young husband they demanded and got a perjured confession stating he'd broken the Virgin Law with his new wife, whom he'd actually met only once at the justice's office. Armed with this confession and a sworn statement from the Baushke girl that the king had never touched her, they got the charges dropped, and the Angelic Messenger was able to return to his kingdom, justifying his flight to the Little People of the sect with Biblical references to Christ's various times of fleeing from his enemies.

The Wade and Baushke troubles weren't the first hints of what went on at Shiloh to leak to the outside world. Two years earlier, in 1908, an Israelite man named Harry Williams had learned about the king's harem and had stormed out of the colony and incited the citizens of Benton Harbor to a murderous fury, leading a lynch mob back to storm Shiloh. The police had stopped and dispersed the mob, but Ben had kept loaded revolvers scattered throughout his headquarters ever since. With the exception of a few Pillars, he'd been unwilling to trust his subjects with the firearms, but he'd had a large locker of leaded clubs installed on the first floor of Jerusalem.

Still, these were merely surface precautions and Ben knew it. What he really needed, re realized, was the good will of the people of Benton Harbor. And as might be expected, the method he chose for winning that good will turned out to be a profitable one.

The House of David had become something of a tourist attraction, with people coming regularly, often from a considerable distance, to see the community of long-haired bearded cultists. Ben had previously discouraged or ignored these intruders. Now, abruptly, he decided to welcome and entertain them. He put his subjects to work clearing the ground behind and beside the Tabernacle, dirictly across the street from Shiloh and Jerusalem. Here he constructed an amusement park, complete with a scale-model miniature railroad, a merry-go-round, chute-the-chutes, a shooting gallery, a photo-while-you-wait stand, an Israelite fortuneteller, a zoo with monkeys and bears, and various other concessions. The creek, which ran through the woods, was dammed up to form a lake and a waterfall. The miniature train, its fare included in the 25¢ admission, circled through the entire site. A lunch stand and a peanut vendor's wagon were added.

King Ben's park was a success from the very day it opened. An excursion boat brought the summer tourists directly across the lake from Chicago, and a street-car ran from the dock to the House of David. Perhaps it was an added attraction for pleasure-seekers to enjoy themselves in the presence of the long-haired cultists to whom all pleasure had been strictly forbidden. At any rate, as many as 200,000 admissions were recorded in a single season. Since everything had been built and was operated by unpaid Flying Rollers, Ben Purnell made an unheard-of profit on this venture.

Of course, since Sunday was the most lucrative day at any amusement park, it became necessary for the Israelites to give up observing the Sabbath.

"Earthly days and nights have lost meaning in the eyes of the Lord now that the final hour is approaching," he assured his followers. "For us, Sunday is just another day. It is all the Sixth Day. So, of course, we continue to labor. But very soon now the books will be sealed and the eternal Seventh Day will begin. Our time of rest and reward is very close at hand."

King Ben was so eager not to lose a single admission fare that he let his park operate full blast even while he was holding his Sunday services and preaching his sermon. From all sides of the Tabernacle, all through his recital of Israelite liturgy, would come the shouts and laughter of the outsiders, the music of the merry-go-round and the shrill penetrating screech of the train whistle. In fact, when movies became popular, he had a projector and a screen installed in his church. The moment the service was finished the Tabernacle became a theatre.

With the income from the park, Ben began buying up common stock in the street-railway systems of both Benton Harbor and nearby St. Joseph. At the same time, he ordered his subjects to start applying for jobs as motormen and conductors. At first the employment office merely laughed at the long-haired bearded men. But when Ben Purnell emerged as the largest single stockholder and began exercising his authority, the hiring policy changed very quickly. Within a few years most of the streetcars of both cities were being operated by Flying Rollers. And King Ben, collecting dividends with one hand and wages with the other, decided that the prophet business was definitely picking up.

"There is no room for idle hands in the Kingdom," he lectured his subjects incessantly.

In addition to holding full-time jobs, the Israelites were required to spend their spare hours and days-off working at the amusement park and at various other projects their king set up for them—a hotel, several hundred acres of farms and orchards, a nursery, a bakery, a toy factory, a candy factory—all of which proved excellent investments when combined with a ready and limitless supply of free labor.

Benjamin Franklin Purnell had come a long way since his days behind the pushcart.

Pleased at the explosive way his fortune was growing, King Ben relaxed his ban on pleasure slightly. Very generously, he ruled that playing baseball was not sinful. Some of his subjects turned out to be quite good at the game and a House of David team was organized. First against other local teams, then against a variety of semi-pro teams from Chicago, finally on a number of nation-wide tours, the bearded long-haired ballplayers somehow managed to nearly always win, usually by one-sided scores.

"None can prevail against the righteous!" Ben would gloat.

Like everything he touched those years, baseball made money for him. Beside the amusement park he had a ball park constructed with a large grandstand. The team that played here each week-end was usually the House of David's second team, since the first team was constantly on tour, but the bleachers were always full.

Even after it was discovered that Ben Purnell was secretly hiring professional ballplayers and giving them wigs and beards to wear, the shrewd Divine Messenger went right on scanning full bleachers and counting his money.

If baseball was profitable, Ben reasoned, basketball might be, too. In much the same manner, a Flying Roller basketball team was organized. The games were, of course, played in the Tabernacle. Backboards and baskets were installed at each end, and the folding chairs were merely moved to the sides before each game.

The House of David hymn-playing band was now expanded into a full-size marching band. Here once again Ben hired professionals and gave them wigs and beards to wear. In fact, it was later testified in court that most of the real Israelites had corks in their horns to prevent their accidentally making any noise with them. Quite often, this band toured the nation with the baseball team.

These tours not only brought in money, but they did a better job of bringing in converts than most of Ben's missionaries. Very quickly, the colony doubled in size, containing, at its peak, 920 adults and numerous children. The remaining woods was soon filled solidly with the little shacks and new clusters of them were built on the various Israelite farm properties. In addition, two large new buildings were constructed near Shiloh and Jerusalem, named The Arc and Bethlehem. Ben even decided that Shiloh wasn't quite enough of a palace for a monarch of his means, and started architects working on the plans for a magnificent new home he would name Diamond House.

Such things as amusement parks, ball teams and marching bands may see like unusual hobbies for a prophet, but King Ben knew exactly what he was doing. This uneducated hillbilly had an instinctive sense of the value of public relations. As the years went by and one morals charge after another was brought against him, local public was usually on his side. Wasn't he one of Benton Harbor's leading businessmen? Didn't he bring in more tourist trade than the city had ever dreamed possible? Hadn't he contributed more than any other man to the growth of Benton Harbor, outstripping the nearby traditional rival of St. Joseph completely?

Besides, how could a man who loved baseball so much ever do the things Ben Purnell was accused of doing?

And the morals charges were bound to come. The bearded king had discovered that the more girls he had to choose from, the more he wanted. The 15 to 20 who had been quartered at Shiloh became 30 and then 40, even reaching a peak of 60 at times, according to the testimony of several witnesses. (By way of comparison, the harem of the Mormon prophet Brigham Young totaled only 28 girls throughout his entire lifetime. In all fairness, however, it should be pointed out that Young fathered some 56 children. Except for Hettie and Coy, and the daughter of his first wife, Angelina, only one other child was definitely credited to King Ben.) The tiny rooms that surrounded the royal apartment, originally designed as single bedrooms, were tightly jammed with tiers of bunks and made to quarter up to three and four girls each.

Just inside the gates of the amusement park, directly above the booth where visitors could obtain pamphlets of Israelite liturgy for whatever they cared to donate, was a colorful life-size painting of King Ben performing an age-old miracle—changing water into wine. The Flying Roller artist who painted it hadn't actually needed too much imagination, for Ben Purnell frequently did perform this miracle. He'd purchased and learned to use the simple magician's apparatus necessary, and it was his favorite way of beginning an evening's relaxation with the girls of Shiloh after a long hard day of managing the complicated business affairs of his rapidly growing empire.

Divinely produced or not, the wine had alcohol in it and the girls got drunk on it. Ben always found them more entertaining after he'd run through this stunt a few times. He liked to sit back in the big throne chair with a half-dozen teen-agers perched about him, petting and fondling them all at once. Many of them were trained as specialists in the art of amusing their king. Lavina Johnson, for example, was the official House of David hula dancer. Ben bought her exotic costumes, paid for her dancing lessons, then used her not only for his own entertainment, but also in the amusement park, on camp-meeting tours and at such House of David exhibits as the one at the Chicago World's Fair.

Sometimes, in the evenings, Ben read aloud from the newspapers to his crowd of harem girls. He read only the stories of murder and rape and other sensational crimes, lecturing the Inner Mystic Circle constantly that the outside world was a cruel and vicious place, reminding them that he had many enemies, that if his enemies ever succeeded in destroying the Seventh Kingdom they would all be left to suffer and starve in the sinful outside world. The one point he constantly stressed was that they must never discuss what went on inside Shiloh with other Israelites and above all with any outsider. His most frequently repeated slogan was "The truth out of season is a lie!"

When King Ben finally felt like retiring and the girls were sent to their rooms, no one knew just who'd be selected as his bed partner that night. Sometimes he'd order a single girl, sometimes two or three; seldom was any one girl called upon more often than once a week. For many years his son Coy was his runner, hurrying down to knock on the chosen girl's door, escorting her back to the royal apartment.

(There used to be a joke about this, commonly heard in Michigan saloons. Coy Purnell, who'd been raised in complete illiteracy, renounced the Israelite faith the moment he was old enough to think for himself, left the colony, cut his hair and died an alcoholic in a Benton Harbor hotel room while still a very young man. King Ben lived on to a ripe old age. According to the barroom philosophers, this was conclusive proof that it isn't the women that kill you, it's running after them.)

Even with all his other activities, Ben Purnell found time to keep up his literary career during these years, turning out *The Ball of Fire, The Flying Roll—Book II,* and several other Sacred Writings. He even edited an official House of David *Vegetarian's Cookbook,* a vast collection of recipes the Little People could use in preparing the cheap simple food allowed them.

In 1912, King Ben bought some 5000 acres on lonely little High Island, in the gull-swept expanses of Northern Lake Michigan. Here he had a summer home built, a structure with a floor plan so unusual that it was known as the Roundhouse among the Israelites. In the center was a large circular room with seven doors, in addition to the one that led out to the porch above the beach. This was Ben's room and around it were seven smaller rooms for the girls, each holding up to four occupants. This was the building the Indians later called the Harem Shack.

King Ben had originally purchased the High Island land as a timber site. But as more and more ground was cleared, he ordered farms established there, keeping a detachment of 30 to 40 Israelite men living the year around at that northern outpost. A number of tarpaper shacks were built there, including a large one with barred windows that served as a prison. Because from the beginning, High Island was the Siberia of Israel. Only those who had somehow offended their king were banished there. Ben Purnell also decided it would be safer to ship the bodies of those who died in the colony up there, rather than go through his usual procedure of claiming they'd doubted or disobeyed him. A local squaw man named Harry Lewis was hired to dispose of them in unmarked graves on a far corner of the island. The winters there were severe. Deaths from starvation and exposure were frequent during the long months of blizzard and constant cold. On several occasions, exiled Israelites attempted to escape across the tricky shifting ice of Lake Michigan and were never seen again.

When World War I broke out in Europe, King Ben decided to stage a spectacular to draw crowds into his amusement park. In the House of David toy factory, he had scale models of an English and a German battleship constructed, each large enough to carry a single passenger, complete with controls and motor-driven propellors and little cannon that actually fired. Then he advertised in the Chicago papers for weeks in advance that on a coming Sunday a realistic sea battle would be held on the artificial pond in the park.

Even though the price of admission was raised that day, the biggest crowd the House of David had even seen showed up, jamming the shores of the pond solidly. It was a thrilling sight—the two battlewagons, perfect in every detail, blasting from every angle, attempting to outmaneuver each other. The cannon were loud and realistic, firing shells that actually exploded when they hit. The ships had been armored heavily enough so that the broadsides they exchanged could not actually penetrate the hulls. But an unforeseen event ended the show in tragedy. One of the battleships rammed the other head-on, sinking it instantly and drowning the unfortunate Israelite trapped inside.

"How do you feel about what happened today?" a newsman demanded of Ben Purnell afterward. "Do you think you were justified in risking and sacrificing the life of one of your own followers just to put on a show?"

"Brother," King Ben told the reporter with a straight face, "if that man had really been living in the True Faith, like he was supposed to, he couldn't possibly have died!"

Twelve

LIKE 1910, 1914 was a time of trouble for Benjamin Franklin Purnell.

"The first time he grabbed me was at an Israelite picnic," a young girl named Augusta Fortney was boldly testifying in a crowded eager-eared courtroom. "I was just fifteen then, and I'd gone off to explore the woods and he'd followed me. I kicked him and got away and ran back to the others. But just a few months later he had a girl named Carrie Ryan bring me into Shiloh. She told me she wanted to show me something. Then he caught me and told her to go watch out the window."

Augusta and her sister were former harem girls who'd fled the House of David and begun talking freely in the outside world. In an attempt to discredit them, King Ben had written an article describing them as a pair of tramps who'd been banished from the Seventh Kingdom for their sins. He'd ordered his son Coy to take it to a Chicago newspaper and to describe himself as the real author. After its publication, the enraged Fortney sisters had sued for slander. Their suit was technically against Coy Purnell. But as the girls told of the life at Shiloh from the witness chair, everyone knew the long-haired king was the real defendant.

At the same time, a man named Mose Clark was suing Ben for seducing his wife.

"He sent me off in the middle of nowhere for two whole years," he was charging in another crowded courtroom, "and when I finally got back, I found out he'd had her living at Shiloh the whole time."

Mose and Edith Clark had joined the colony early in 1912. The king had allowed them to go on living together, but he'd ordered them to obey the Virgin Law strictly. Mose had been given work on the big farm. Edith had been assigned to sweeping and dusting the business offices at Shiloh.

One day she'd accidentally opened a wrong door and seen the Seventh Divine Messenger in bed with a girl named Leah Wright.

"Well, Sister Clark," Ben had chuckled, "either come on in and join us or else close the door."

Edith had turned and run out of the building, back across the amusement park and through the woods to her cottage. Thinking it over, Ben Purnell had decided she'd most likely tell her husband. He'd called in Francis Thorpe, his executive secretary.

"Go out to the farm, get Mose Clark and bring him straight to me!" he'd ordered the little man.

Then he'd sent for Esther Johnson, his trusted Girl Friday.

"Go stay with the Clark woman until you hear from me," he'd told her. "Don't let her talk to anyone."

When Thorpe had brought in Mose Clark, Ben had told him he'd been chosen for the new detachment being sent to High Island.

"These are the Pioneers of Israel," he'd intoned. "This is a very great honor, especially for a newcomer like yourself."

"Edith coming with me?"

"You and the other Pioneers must first prepare suitable shelter. Would you want your wife to suffer in the wilderness?"

Mose Clark had let himself be rushed aboard the *Rising Sun* without even a chance to say good-bye to Edith. His first winter on High Island had been a terrible one, with the freeze-up coming early and catching the detachment short of food, with some men dying of starvation and others disappearing in attempts to cross the ice.

When spring had finally come and the schooner had reached the outpost, Edith Clark had not been aboard. All of Mose's attempts to see the bearded king, vacationing just a short distance away with a select group of the girls of Shiloh, had failed. Another severe winter had closed down. One spring night, Mose had finally slipped off in a small skiff, working his way southward on a lake boat and hurrying back to the House of David to find his wife.

Only then had he learned that Edith had been part of the Inner Mystic Circle ever since he'd left. The king had ordered her out of their little shack and into Shiloh. He'd worked on her incessantly with Israelite doctrine, explaining that blood-purification was absolutely essential to salvation, that only the Divine Messenger could sow the seeds of purity. With such persistence, he'd eventually worn out her resistance.

Mose Clark blamed his wife for not putting up more of a fight and filed for divorce, charging Ben with seducing her. As a result of this and the publicity from the Fortney suit, both the Federal government and the State of Michigan launched investigations.

Once again, the long-haired prophet sped off for Canada, taking only two girls with him in his shiny black new limousine. For Ben Purnell, this was roughing it.

Once again, the entire Inner Mystic Circle was married off to guard against the possibility of medical examinations, with Esther Johnson and her new assistant Edith Meldrum arranging the mass-production weddings. As an added precaution they shipped all the harem girls up to High Island for the summer. Then the intricate under-cover work of battling the four threats to the Seventh Kingdom began.

Esther perjured herself uninhibitedly in refuting the Fortney charges against her king, blackening the character of the two sisters with a number of stories she later admitted were lies. She made a special trip to Big Rapids in an attempt to convince Governor Ferris that all the charges against the House of David were nothing more than the result of religious prejudices. Potential witnesses were blackmailed with confessions they'd written, forced to give sworn statements exonerating King Ben of any wrongdoing. Some were bought off with sizable cash bribes. Local public officials were reminded that the king had a thousand votes in his pocket and urged to use their influence in his behalf.

With the facts hopelessly clouded in their case, the Fortney girls were awarded only a token judgment of six cents. With his wife afraid to testify against the king, the Mose Clark suit did no damage. Finding insufficient evidence, the Federal government dropped its investigation and the State of Michigan followed suit.

The In-gathering of Israel had weathered the most severe storm yet.

But Ben Purnell had been deeply worried. Upon his return he put a crew of his subjects to work digging an elaborate series of tunnels beneath the colony buildings, complete with secret entrances. He ordered a recently converted electrician named Swanson to plan and install a raid-warning device with buzzers and flashing lights, an ingenious system by which sentries at various points on the outskirts of the colony could alert him instantly, no matter where he happened to be, if mobs or warrant servers showed up.

And yet, actually, the bearded prophet had learned nothing from his year of constant trouble. While electrician Swanson was busy working on the wiring, Benjamin Franklin Purnell amused himself by cleansing the blood of his 20-year-old wife Ruth.

About this time, King Ben had a different kind of trouble, one that would naturally become an obsession with a man of his vanity—his hair was turning gray. Afraid this could cast doubt on his claim of being immortal, he had a number of hairdressers work on him in secret. An honest beautician told him the truth.

"The only way you'll even hide those streaks is by dyeing it all black!"

Sorrowfully, King Ben gave in, first preparing his subjects for the transformation by announcing this in advance as a miraculous omen that the Millennium was now very close at hand.

Young Coy Purnell renounced the Israelite faith and fled the colony soon after the Fortney suit. His mother was heartbroken. She began slipping large amounts of money out to him, giving him enough so that he started dressing in flashy clothes, entertaining a wild crowd of young friends and drinking heavily. Discovering this, the king ordered his wife to stop.

For the first time in their life together, Mary stood up to Ben.

"You drove him away!" she accused. "You took that girl he liked, that Gladys Hill, and put her in Shiloh with the rest of them. You got him mixed up in all that court trouble. Well, I'll go on giving him whatever I please. This happens to be a community-property state. You try to stop me, I'll see a lawyer about it."

King Ben was trapped. He'd originally organized the House of David as a church corporation in order to take advantage of tax laws. The State of Michigan had ruled that the colony was engaging in too many business activities to be considered a church, and Ben had put everything in his own name.

"I have been harboring a scorpion," he complained sadly and helplessly to his harem girls.

For comfort in her grief at losing her last child, Mary

Purnell began turning more and more often to Francis Thorpe, Ben's executive secretary. Considering her age, this may have been nothing more than a close friendship, although a number of Israelites later described it in court as an affair. With all the young ladies at Shiloh to pick from, the loss of his wife's affection still angered Ben.

"Mary's Little Lamb!" he called Thorpe in disgust.

Realizing her power and flaunting her independence, the Queen, who on occasion had even helped procure the girls, now began to object to the King's harem excesses. Ben had gotten into the habit of taking a crowd of Inner Circle members with him wherever he went— to his office, through the colony grounds, to the amusement park, on inspection tours of his farms and orchards and factories, even to downtown Benton Harbor to the block of business buildings he'd purchased there. He'd also started fondling and kissing them whenever and wherever the whim seized him. Abruptly, Mary told him to start acting with a little more royal dignity.

"Benjamin had better begin watching his step around here!" several different Flying Rollers later quoted her.

The long-haired prophet had developed a hundred cunning ways of fighting court charges and government investigations. But there was no way for him to combat this annoyance. He could only curse beneath his breath and bear it.

In 1915, according to the later sworn testimony of a number of Israelite witnesses, a forced initiation into the Inner Mystic Circle ended in tragedy.

"He's not a Divine Being at all!" a young girl named Eliza Murphy blurted out to her mother. "He started pulling off my clothes, and when I fought back he twisted my arms behind me and—"

"Not another word!" Mrs. Murphy clamped a hand over the girl's mouth and shook her angrily. "Don't you dare talk like that about King Benjamin! Don't you ever let me hear you say such things again!"

"But it's the truth!" Eliza broke free, sobbing. She was

a small thin-boned girl who looked even younger than her 15 years. "I swear to God it is!"

"You listen to me!" Her mother's face was dark and twisted with rage. "If you want to get yourself banished from the kingdom, if you want to burn with the rest of the world, there's no way I can stop you. But keep that evil talk away from me! I want to stay here!"

Eliza was forcibly returned to Shiloh, where Cora Mooney angrily ordered her to her room. And then the High Priestess questioned her mother suspiciously.

"What did she tell you?"

"Oh, nothing. She was just a little homesick, I guess."

"Was she making up lies about Benjamin?" Cora Mooney asked bluntly.

"Well," Mrs. Murphy hesitated, "I don't think—"

"Several of the girls have been doing that lately. It seems to be a conspiracy among them. They don't want to settle down and learn the principles of the Sacred Writings, so they've made up some vicious stories among themselves and threatened to tell them if they're forced to study. They may be too young to realize what a blasphemous thing they're doing, but we certainly can't permit it."

"I think she must have just had a bad dream," Mrs. Murphy pleaded weakly.

"If you hear evil talk and fail to report it, you share the full guilt!" the High Priestess warned her. "Now what did Eliza tell you?"

"She's really a good girl. She wouldn't—"

"*What did she say?*" Cora Mooney shouted.

"Well . . . that King Benjamin was . . . doing things to her . . . things a mortal man might do. But don't worry. I brought her back and I made her promise . . ."

"All right," the High Priestess interrupted her. "You can go now. But if you hear evil talk again, you're to report it immediately!"

After Mrs. Murphy had left, beefy thick-set Cora Mooney took from a desk drawer an object that seemed strangely out of place in that world of bearded men—

a razor strop. Then she went up the stairs to the young Murphy girl's room.

When the first piercing screams split the midday quiet of Shiloh, most of the second-floor girls merely cowered in their rooms. But a few like Hazel Ruth Wade and a girl named Gladys Bamford hurried down the hall and pounded on the bolted door. Then Esther Johnson and an older office worker named Estelle Meldrum came rushing up the stairs to join them.

"What's going on?" they demanded, when Cora Mooney opened the door and closed it behind her, dimming the sound of steady sobbing there. The leather strop still hung from her hand.

"I've just been giving Eliza Murphy a little something she had coming," the High Priestess told them calmly. "She was telling lies about Benjamin."

But even after the beating the little Murphy girl remained rebellious. None of the bearded king's arguments, none of his promises of eternal life or his threats of eternal damnation, could persuade her to give in to his purification rites. Eliza fought him with all the strength in her slim body. Only by direct brutal force was the long-haired prophet able to see that her blood was properly cleansed.

He took her along on his last vacation trip to High Island that year. And when she still remained stubborn there in the Roundhouse, he decided that an even stronger form of discipline was needed. There was another rebel in his harem at the time, a girl named Jessie Wheeler. As he was preparing to sail for Benton Harbor, he took the two of them aside.

"I've been extremely patient with you both," he told them, "but your attitude toward the purification rites is open sacrilege and heresy, and this cannot be tolerated any longer. You'll promise me now that you'll perform these rites in the future with the proper respect and humility, or else you'll remain here on the island for the winter!"

The two girls faced him in stubborn silence.

"All right!" he muttered grimly. "We'll see!"

Benjamin Franklin Purnell was certain that when he returned in the spring he'd find this pair thoroughly chastised, ready to submit humbly to his ministering, ready to show some appreciation for the advantages life at Shiloh offered over the life the rank-and-file Israelites led. But it didn't work out quite that way.

There in the Siberia of Israel, with only the banished, the aged and the insane for company, where driven snow swirled incessantly, where the wind shrieked like a screaming girl and stabbed relentlessly through the crude tarpaper shacks, the two teen-age Israelites lost all interest in both the promised eternal life to come and the life here and now. They found a sack of the white powdered arsenic used to spray the vegetable gardens, mixed it with water, closed their eyes and swallowed it quickly.

Jessie Wheeler choked on the milk-colored fluid, threw most of it back up, and suffered only severe stomach cramps. Eliza Murphy kept it down. And on the far side of the island, King Ben's hired squaw man chopped out another unmarked grave in the frozen ground.

In 1916, Ben Purnell did a very foolish, childish thing. Hazel Ruth Wade—"Salvation Nell"—had been religiously obeying his commandments through the half-dozen years that had gone by since her forced marriage to Irving Smith. She'd humbly submitted to his booster shots of blood-cleansing. She'd worked the countryside tirelessly in search of converts for him, with Irving driving the team and setting up the platform and torches for her camp meetings. Living together in a small covered wagon on one tour after another, the young couple had religiously obeyed their king's Virgin Law.

But one night on the road, happy and excited after an unusually successful meeting, Hazel Ruth impulsively embraced Irving and kissed him on the cheek.

He pushed her away, stared at her in horror, then broke out sobbing.

"What have you done?" he cried, again and again. "What have you done?"

Sick inside with guilt and fear, Hazel Ruth still tried to comfort him.

"It was my fault, all my fault, and I'll say so when I confess it," she promised him.

Tormented by visions of eternal punishment, they gave up the tour and turned back for Benton Harbor the next morning, hardly speaking to each other throughout the long trip. Upon her return, Hazel Ruth wrote out a full confession of the incident.

If King Ben had used the same shrewdness in managing his harem that he used in business matters, he'd have quietly forgiven the girl and retained her loyalty. But by this time, the mere thought of another man as much as touching one of his girls was enough to send him into a blind unreasoning rage.

"An act of lust!" he shouted. "A contemptible bestial act of lust!"

The incident became an insane fixation with him. At the next service, his voice thundering above the noises of the busy amusement park, he ordered her to her feet and gave her an unmerciful tongue-lashing. The entire colony began turning their heads when she approached, refusing to answer her greeting.

Heartbroken, Hazel Ruth Wade fled into the evil and sinful outside world.

Once among normal people, the shy little hymn singer soon realized just how much of a dupe she'd been. Living with her sister Edna for a time, then visiting her father in Indiana, she came to look upon the dozen years she'd spent in the colony as an incredible nightmare. In 1917 she returned to Benton Harbor, unafraid, determined to get her kid sister Cleatus out of Ben's clutches.

Something about this previously timid and soft-voiced girl worried the bearded king so much that he stayed out of town during her return. He had Esther Johnson get a statement exonerating him of any wrong doing from Cleatus. He desperately wanted a similar statement from Hazel Ruth. But even though the offer was raised to several thousand dollars, Salvation Nell wasn't buying it.

The moment her sister was safe, she went all the way to Washington, camped on President Wilson's doorstep until he gave her an audience, then told him exactly what was going on at the House of David.

Woodrow Wilson listened politely, but turned the matter over to his secretary Joseph Tumulty. Tumulty sent the girl to the Justice Department, where she was merely referred from one office to another until she finally gave up.

The Federal government had a few more serious things to worry about at the time than a fake prophet keeping a harem in a small Michigan city. The United States of America had just gone to war.

When the first draft boards were set up, King Ben promptly notified them that his domain was a separate kingdom owing allegiance only to God and that his subjects were not subject to conscription. The government failed to agree with this and drafted the Israelites anyway. Furious at being robbed of a good share of his labor supply, Ben Purnell made the most of the situation.

Once again, he married off his entire current harem to young Flying Roller men. But this group marriage had a different purpose than the earlier ones. All through the war, some fifty or more allotment checks were dropped into the mailbox at Shiloh each month to be promptly endorsed by the Inner Circle members and promptly cashed by their lord and master.

You had to get up pretty early in the morning to beat old King Ben.

Thirteen

ON A spring day in 1919, a commotion broke out at the House of David amusement park.

As the tourists and pleasure-seekers crowded about to watch, the kindly little old lady who tended the curio stand suddenly began shouting at a pretty teen-age girl, grabbing both her shoulders and shaking her again and again. This was Mrs. Isabelle Pritchard, the Australian widow to whose daughters King Ben had promised to be a father.

"You're lying!" the gray-haired woman shrieked. "You know you're lying!"

"It's true, Mama!" the young girl cried. "That's what he did!"

"To Irene, too?"

Choking and sobbing, Hilda Pritchard nodded.

Her face dark with anger, Mrs. Pritchard snatched up one of the small cheap Bibles sold at her concession.

"Here! You put your hand on this! Now you swear to me, you swear with God for a witness, that you're telling me the truth!"

"I swear it, Mama!" The girl was hysterical now. "That's what happened!"

For a moment, the little old lady seemed about to collapse. She set the Bible back on the counter and shook her head slowly, breathing very had.

"Then it's true!" she gasped softly. "I know how I raised you. You wouldn't lie on the Book. It must be true."

She hesitated for a long time, then suddenly straightened up, her face dark with rage again.

"Come on!"

Grabbing Hilda by the wrist, she dragged her out from behind the stand and bulled her way directly through the growing crowd with her head lowered, shouldering and elbowing the curious onlookers aside. As she went out through the gates of the park and directly across the street toward the business offices of Shiloh, the outsiders swarmed after her to see the fun.

Inside the office, Esther Johnson and Edith Meldrum tried to stop her, but she forced her way into each of the rooms and then started upstairs, the teen-age girl still in tow behind her.

"Where's Ben?" she shouted at everyone. "I want to see Ben! Right now!"

The king wasn't in Shiloh, not in his quarters or any of the adjacent rooms. Keeping her hand locked tightly about her daughter's wrist, Isabelle Pritchard slammed back downstairs and out of the building. The crowd tagged along as she hurried past the arch to search Jerusalem, once again forcing her way into every room.

"Where's that old fraud hiding?" she demanded of Queen Mary and Cora Mooney, as they stared at her, shocked and indignant. "He might as well come out! I'll find him!"

Finally she headed down the street and over the beautifully landscaped grounds of the magnificent new Diamond House, now in the last stages of completion. Still hoping to see the fun, the crowd swarmed after her, trampling down the new evergreens and shrubs and flower beds.

Two Pillars tried to stop the enraged woman at the door. Without relaxing her grip on her daughter, she smashed one in the stomach with her elbow, leaving him doubled up and choking for breath. She locked her fingers in the beard of the other, yanked him forward to trip and fall across the first, then went on in with the crowd cheering her on.

She caught Ben Purnell just inside the big entrance hall, coming out to see what all the noise was about.

"You sneaking old goat!" she shrieked at him. "You're as phony as your dyed hair!"

"Keep your voice down!" he urged her, noticing the audience on the porch.

"Keep my voice down? I came halfway around the world to find the True Faith! You took all my money! You ruined my girls! Now you tell me to keep my voice down!"

"Don't make a scene here!" he ordered her.

"I'll make a scene, all right, you old fraud! The Son of Man, are you? Well, I'll Son of Man you, you son-of-a—"

With a loud explosive crack, she hauled off and slammed

him across the face. He caught her arm just as she was about to swing again. She let go of Hilda's wrist and brought the other hand up to claw at his eyes like a wildcat.

His patience exhausted, King Ben had just drawn back his arm and doubled up his fist to strike her when he realized that the crowd was surging through the door and moving in on him menacingly. He turned and pulled free with the scratching, hair- and beard-pulling woman chasing after him. Hitting an alarm button, he raced up the stairs to take refuge in a second-floor room, latching the door behind him.

A well-drilled force of long-haired young men appeared almost instantly, armed with leaded clubs, politely but firmly suggesting that the trespassers return to the amusement park. The Pritchard widow was also reminded that she had no business here, reminded by a frozen-faced Pillar who had her escorted from Diamond House by a pair of husky Israelites who locked her arms tightly and ignored her violent threats.

"I'm not through with that old goat yet!" she promised them. "Not by a long shot!"

She hurried to find Irene, who was working as the king's personal cook. She rushed both girls out of the colony. Then she went into circuit court with a morals complaint, charging the bearded prophet with raping her daughters.

There had been too many such complainants for this charge to be passed off lightly—Mrs. Lulu Baushke, the Fortney girls, Mose Clark. And yet, while Ben Purnell took another quick Canadian vacation, his lieutenants prepared a defense that was extremely effective. His attorney introduced into evidence several hundred signed statements, one from every Israelite female above the age of puberty, each testifying to the king's absolute purity of conduct.

The Pritchard charges were smothered by the sheer weight of numbers. The Seventh Kingdom had weathered still another storm.

But even so, these were the twilight years for the god-king. For the following year he made the serious mistake of turning Esther Johnson against him.

No one had served the bearded prophet more faithfully than this trim-figured little Swedish woman, now 30 years of age. She'd tricked and bribed and blackmailed his accusers. She'd silenced rebellion within his domain by a wide variety of underhanded intrigues. He'd reserved only the most delicate assignments for her and she'd never failed him.

Ben's attorneys later claimed that his quarrel with his Girl Friday began when he refused her a thousand dollars she wanted to take a business course at a nearby college. Esther herself insisted that the quarrel grew out of her friendship for an Israelite family who'd become disillusioned and were preparing to leave the colony, a family whose son she later married. Chances are that still another factor was involved. King Ben had the foolish habit of letting his current harem favorite indulge her every whim. Most likely, some 15- or 16-year-old, jealous and resentful of Esther Johnson's power and authority in the cult, poisoned the prophet's mind against her.

Whatever the original cause of the argument, a morning came when Esther found herself locked out of her own private office.

"I want to see Benjamin!" she told his new executive secretary, H. T. DeWhirst, firmly. "I think he knows better than this."

DeWhirst shook his head coldly. He was a newcomer to the sect, a former circuit-court judge from Redlands, California, a former Methodist Sunday-school teacher, a former head of the local Y.M.C.A. Upon being converted and arriving at the House of David, his first work assignment had been picking up waste paper on the amusement park grounds. But his rise to power had been almost as rapid as Esther Johnson's fall from power. King Benjamin's health had been failing rapidly. An old fall from a horse had been troubling him lately. In addition, the doctors he'd been secretly consulting had found him suffering seriously from tuberculosis. More and more, he'd been delegating the work of running his kingdom. More and more, he'd come to depend upon Judge DeWhirst.

"Benjamin is unable to see anyone today," the judge told her. "Benjamin isn't feeling too well."

"He'll feel a lot worse before I'm done with him!" Esther promised.

She returned to her room and found Cora Mooney waiting for her there.

"Benjamin has decided he wants this wing remodeled," the High Priestess of Shiloh, who'd been with the prophet since Fostoria, announced. "He wishes you to move out to the big farm for a while."

"I see," Esther said softly. The only living quarters at the farm were tarpaper shacks. This was banishment.

"The truth of the matter is you're no longer welcome here," Cora Mooney said haughtily. "You may as well realize it."

Esther turned and stared at her a moment.

"I don't like your tone of voice," she decided.

"What you like or don't like isn't quite as important around here as it once was."

"Isn't it?" Esther Johnson smiled dangerously. "Do you have any idea just how much I know about this place and everyone in it? You're not talking to little Eliza Murphy now!"

"Who—who's Eliza Murphy?" The High Priestess' voice was faltering and unconvincing.

"Come now!" Esther's laugh was crisp and deadly. "I know all the details and I can prove them. I even know where she's buried. Now what were you saying to me?"

"It's not my fault," Cora Mooney whined. "I'm just obeying Benjamin's commandments."

"Well, you go right on obeying them if you like. But you be a little more careful how you talk to me. Is that clear?"

The High Priestess merely nodded in silence.

"All right. Now get out of here. I want to pack."

Esther Johnson had seen this moment coming on for months, and she'd secreted a number of important papers to take with her. She moved to Grand Rapids, divorced the husband given to her in the 1910 group marriages, and married the son of the apostate Israelite family she'd befriended. Preparing detailed and documented evidence, she encouraged her father-in-law to sue for every cent he'd originally turned in to the House of David, plus interest and wages for the time he'd worked in the colony.

In 1923, a judgment of $24,000 was returned. For the very first time in his two-decade reign, a case against King Ben had held up in court.

That same year, two young sisters named Ruth and Gladys Bamford swore out rape charges against the long-haired prophet and sued him for $200,000. With Ruth Bamford, Ben Purnell's harem had completed the full cycle of a generation. She'd been born in the colony, less than a month after her mother had entered in 1907.

The story the Bamford girls told from the witness stand had a familiar ring. Their father had died of pneumonia in a poorly heated shack and King Ben had promised he'd be a father to them. Their mother now appeared as a defense witness to profess her faith in the prophet and to swear her daughters were lying.

In both the 1923 trials, Hazel Ruth Wade offered her services as a plaintiff's witness. In neither of these civil suits did Ben Purnell actually show up to defend himself.

As a matter of fact, it was suddenly realized that no outsider had seen King Ben since October of 1922.

The weight of public opinion had finally become too great to be ignored. Editorial writers throughout the entire state were screaming for the bearded monarch's scalp. The Detroit *Free Press* led the attack, running one front-page exposé after another, and newspapers the nation over began carrying the stories. Demands for action poured onto the governor's desk and rang out in the legislative chambers. A grand jury was hastily convened and a standing warrant for his arrest was issued.

But when a surprise raid was made on the House of

David, there was no sign of King Ben. Judge DeWhirst and the other Pillars blandly told reporters he'd gone up to heaven in a flaming chariot like Elijah.

The State of Michigan answered this by putting a $3000 price on his head.

Tips were checked out by the thousands. Raid after raid was made on the colony. Israelite life went on as usual—the amusement park ran full blast, the baseball team thrilled local crowds and toured the country, the factories and farms kept on producing. But the long-haired bearded king was nowhere to be found.

Then reports came drifting in from out of the country. Someone had seen him in Canada. He was in London. He was founding a new kingdom in New Zealand, Australia, Tokyo, Paris, Berlin.

For nearly four full years, the police of the entire world hunted King Ben in vain.

Then a new rumor came out of nowhere and began spreading rapidly.

"He's dead!" citizens of Benton Harbor would laughingly tell reporters. "Of course, he's dead. He's been dead for years. But only Queen Mary and DeWhirst and a few others even know about it. They're keeping it from the rest because King Ben's supposed to be immortal and they're all supposed to attain immortality if they believe in him. If they knew he was dead, the colony would go to pieces overnight."

The rumor made sense. In the time between his last public appearance and the issuing of the standing warrant for his arrest, every reporter who'd attempted to interview him had been politely escorted about the colony by Judge DeWhirst. References to the king had been commonly heard—he wasn't feeling well this morning, he'd just left to drive out to the big farm, he couldn't see anyone today, but maybe tomorrow. Telephone calls, supposedly to the king, were invariably made in front of newsmen. But no one had actually seen him.

The rumor not only made sense, it made a beautiful human-interest story—a colorful religious sect held together only by a belief in the immortality of a man who was actually long dead. More and more newspapers began dignifying the rumor in print. Bit by bit, the long fruitless hunt for the king slowed to a halt. The authorities also began accepting the theory that he'd been dead for years.

Suddenly, in mid-November of 1926, the Detroit *Free Press* received what was first regarded as a crank letter. A girl named Bessie Daniels, claiming to be a former Inner Circle member who'd just recently left the colony, told the fantastic story that King Ben was very much alive, that he'd never left the House of David, much less the country, that he'd been hiding in the colony itself for more than four years.

The letter was checked out by state troopers as a matter of routine, just as the thousands of earlier tips had been checked.

"How could he hide there this long?" the officers demanded.

"He's in Diamond House," Bessie Daniels told them. "He had it built with secret rooms and passageways and hidden doorways and he's got an electric warning system."

"Who knows he's there?"

"At least half the people in the colony."

"We've had that place watched day after day for years. You say he had a bunch of young girls sent to him every night? Our men would have noticed anything like that."

"Sometimes they dressed us up like old women and had us hunch over when we walked and we went in one at a time. Sometimes we took mops and brooms and buckets and pretended we were a cleaning crew."

"Old King Ben would be somewhere in his mid-sixties if he's still alive. Are you actually trying to tell us that little more than a year ago he was still . . . he still wanted whole bunches of girls sent over every night?"

Bessie Daniels blushed. "I can't help how old he was. He still wanted us sent over, all right!"

"Young lady, do you realize how many times that place was raided and searched?"

"Sure. And I think he was tipped off every time. I saw Queen Mary talking with the sheriff after one of those raids and I heard her say, "There's a thousand votes right here we can swing any way we like and don't you forget it!"

The amazed officer looked at the other troopers and scratched his head.

"I'll be darned if I don't believe her!"

He rose to his feet and his voice was crisp and efficient. "All right. We're going out there right now, and there'll be no tip-off this time."

Just a little before midnight, several carloads of police screeched to a stop in front of Diamond House. The heavily bolted doors were smashed in with axes. In the dimly lit interior, a woman was seen running upstairs. The troopers quickly overtook her, then followed the Daniels girl's directions through an invisible door in the wall and along a hidden passageway cleverly built into the shell of the mansion.

Deep in a secret system of rooms, the 65-year-old king was trapped in bed. With him in her nightgown was Myrtle Tulk, who claimed to be his nurse. Also with him and similarly dressed, with no such explanation for their presence, were two teen-age girls. Blinking and cursing as cameras flashed in his face, snarling like an old bear brought to bay, Benjamin Franklin Purnell was hauled off to jail.

The long hunt was over.

Fourteen

IT WAS the trial of the century. It lasted more than three months, covering 51 actual days of testimony. And on a good share of those 51 days, the stories of Ben Purnell's villainy ran side by side with the stories of Charles Lindbergh's heroism on the front pages of the nation's newspapers. Five hundred exhibits were introduced; 225 witnesses were called.

His once-powerful body so wasted by tuberculosis that he weighed a mere 100 pounds, his once-striking red-gold hair so hopelessly faded to gray that he no longer bothered dyeing it black, King Ben was brought in on a stretcher to lay there and listen in silence while an endless parade of witnesses recounted nearly every sin of his busy lifetime—his 23 years of rule at Benton Harbor, his days at Fostoria, his pushcart and covered-wagon travels, his part in the Detroit colony, his wanderings as a street preacher, his life as a hobo. Even Angelina, the wife he hadn't seen in 48 years, managed to testify against him.

"What was he doing while he was married to you?" George Nichols, the special prosecutor spearheading the attack for the attorney general's office, asked the little old mountain lady.

"Nothin'," she told him. "Jes' livin' off my father."

"It has been claimed that Benjamin Purnell was an industrious young broom-maker in his youth. Was he a broom-maker when he was living with you?"

"Naw. He never made no brooms. Never while I knowed him."

The first day of the trial—May 16, 1927—had been devoted entirely to the prosecution's opening statement. Although three criminal charges of rape, brought by Ruth and Gladys Bamford and Bessie Daniels, were pending against King Ben, the State of Michigan had decided to concentrate its first and primary effort in a suit to have the House of David abolished as a menace to public morals. It was on the second day that Angelina took the stand. In a surprise move the prosecution also called a number of hostile witnesses—Flying Rollers John Synder and Silas Mooney, even Queen Mary herself.

"Isn't it true," Nichols demanded of her, "that both you and Benjamin were part of the notorious Prince Michael Mills colony in Detroit, both before and after the Prince was sent to prison on morals charges nearly thirty-five years ago?"

"Oh, no!" Queen Mary insisted. "We were never part of that group."

"You are on a witness stand and you are under oath!" the state's attorney reminded her.

"We may have stopped in for a few days just once on a preaching tour."

"There are still a number of members of that colony living who can be brought in as witnesses," George Nichols warned her.

"It's hard to remember that long ago. It may have been longer than just a few days. As a matter of fact, I think that was where the Spirit first came to Benjamin."

"Isn't it true that he was a Pillar of that colony, that he was one of the Prince's closest advisors?"

"Your honor," Queen Mary turned to Judge Louis H. Fead, "I refuse to testify against my husband!"

"Your honor," Nichols countered, "Benjamin Purnell is not her husband and we can prove it." He turned back to Mary. "When were you married to him? Where?"

"The time and place of our marriage is a secret between Benjamin and myself!"

The prosecutor introduced documentary evidence showing her husband's marriage to Angelina had never been dissolved. Then he dropped the point and introduced records, supplied by Esther Johnson, of 10 Israelites who'd been secretly buried on High Island without any coroner ever issuing a death certificate.

But these were merely preliminaries, warming-up exercises for the long hard fight that lay ahead. On the third day the prosecutor got down to the real business of the trial and set the pattern for the rest of the proceedings by calling a former harem girl to the stand—Mrs. Ruth Swanson, the wife of the electrician who'd installed King Ben's raid-warning system.

"How long did you live in the House of David?" George Nichols asked her.

"About a year," she remembered. "We sold our house

in Florida and turned in all of the money, about thirteen thousand dollars."

"When was that?"

"We came in nineteen-thirteen and left in nineteen-fourteen."

"Were you and your husband allowed to go on living together at the colony?"

"No. He lived out at the big farm with a bunch of other men. I was working in the office at Shiloh and I had a room right behind it on the first floor."

"Did you ever go upstairs?"

"Yes."

"When was that?"

"In the early fall of nineteen-thirteen. It was right after the big Federal white-slavery investigation. All the girls from the second floor had been taken up to High Island and the place was almost deserted."

"Will you tell us what happened?"

"Well, I always kept the door to my room locked because it was near the entrance to the street. Then one time Myrtle Tulk came and knocked about midnight. She said the girls were coming back from High Island, that my room was needed and I had to go upstairs."

"What did you say to that?"

"I told her I'd be glad to share my room with other girls. She went away, then came back and said no, Benjamin said I had to go upstairs."

"Did you go then?"

"Yes."

"And what happened?"

"Well, I'd only been in bed upstairs a little while when the door opened and King Benjamin walked in. He sat down on the bed and talked for a long time."

"What did he talk about?"

"About the Israelite faith, about how to attain immortality, about the importance of blood-purification."

"Then what happened?"

Ruth Swanson hesitated for a long time, her face reddening. "Well . . . I thought he was telling the truth," she finally said. She shook her head slowly. "I actually thought that in submitting to him I was doing the proper thing—what God wanted me to do."

"How did you happen to leave the colony?"

"I finally got up enough nerve to tell my husband about it. He took me away right then and there."

"And was the money you'd brought with you when you joined returned when you left?"

"No. We just got ten dollars and train tickets to Chicago."

"Thank you, Mrs. Swanson." George Nichols turned back to his seat. "Your witness."

William J. Barnard, the chief defense lawyer, bore down on the witness with an angry look on his face. He was an attorney every bit as famous as the great Colonel Atkinson had been a generation earlier, given to spectacular courtroom antics. The long-haired bearded Judge DeWhirst was helping to mastermind the strategy from the defense-counsel table. But on the floor this was almost strictly Bill Barnard's show.

"Isn't it true," he loudly demanded of Mrs. Swanson, "that upon leaving Benton Harbor you and your husband both signed an affidavit releasing the House of David from any claim upon it?"

"Yes. We had to."

"Oh? You had to! Isn't it also true," he shouted at her, "that you signed other affidavits swearing that the House of David was a moral place?"

"Yes."

"Yes!" He waved his finger directly in her face. "And so now you've come all the way back from Florida to tell an entirely different story. Why? Who contacted you and asked you to come?"

"Well, Esther Johnson—"

"Esther Johnson, huh? So Esther Johnson brought you in here with this story. How much money did she promise you?"

"Just our expenses. She said the State would pay—"

"Isn't it true," he shouted at the top of his lungs, "that the only reason you're here telling this fantastic story is that if the House of David is abolished and its property sold, you're hoping for some of the proceeds?"

"No!" the woman sobbed. "I'm here because I don't want what happened to me to happen to some other—"

"No more questions!" Barnard contemptuously turned his back on her and strode back to his seat.

The prosecution then varied its attack by calling three men to the stand—Ruth Swanson's husband, who backed up her story; Hicks Vaughan, who told a typical tale of having his wife and daughters separated from him and his family destroyed after joining the colony; and Herbert Yogeler, who testified about his forced marriage to Vaughan's daughter Mildred. The defense accused all three of wanting the colony abolished to share in the proceeds. On May 19, another girl who'd served in Ben Purnell's harem was called—the former Dolly Smith, now married, still an extremely attractive woman at 33.

"When were you first sent to live at Shiloh?" Prosecutor Nichols asked her.

"In nineteen-nine, when I was fifteen."

"Will you tell us what happened?"

"Well, Lillie Birkman, a girl I'd been friends with, took me to King Benjamin's apartment. He fussed around with her for a while so I wouldn't be afraid. Then he took me on his lap and had Lillie pull down the shades. Then she left."

There was a long period of heavy silence.

"Were you forced to submit to him that night?" George Nichols prompted her.

"Yes."

"And how long were you kept at Shiloh for immoral purposes?"

"About three years. Then I was sent out on missionary duty."

"How many girls were in Benjamin Purnell's harem at this time?"

"Around thirty."

"Were there favorites among them?"

"I think Toots Sassman was his favorite, although Harriet Baushke was quite a pet. But he kept Myrtle Tulk and May Cardle in the room next to him."

On cross-examination, the now-familiar accusation that this girl and the others were conspiring to have the House of David abolished and share in its wealth was heard.

"If all this really happened, why is it that you waited nearly twenty years to tell anyone about it? Why didn't you go to the police long ago?"

"What good would it have done?" Dolly Smith yelled back. "Hazel Ruth Wade went all the way to Washington and saw the President and what good did it do? King Benjamin had them all paid off, right on up to the top!"

On that note, Judge Fead adjourned the case until the following Thursday. As the army of newsmen scrambled to file their stories, several of them, seeking a new angle, caught the long-haired bearded Judge H. T. DeWhirst and interviewed him on the courthouse steps.

"Will King Ben appear to testify and answer these charges?" they asked. Ben Purnell had been released on $10,000 bail.

"He most certainly will . . . providing his doctors permit it, of course."

"Is it true that he originally set the date of the Millennium at nineteen-hundred-and-six?" a reporter asked.

"Of course not," DeWhirst laughed.

"I've seen a copy of one of his Sacred Writings," the reporter persisted, "and that was the date given there."

"Oh, yes," the bearded judge smiled. "Benjamin has explained that to us. It was a printer's error."

When court reconvened on May 26, the State of Michigan called its star witness to the stand—the former Esther Johnson. And among the veteran trial reporters in the press section, it was the general opinion that the prosecution's case rested directly on her slim, narrow shoulders, on how well she'd hold up under the hard-hitting cross-examination of the famed Bill Barnard.

For years, Esther had campaigned against the House of David. It was she who'd gone about the country rounding up witnesses and urging them to come back to testify. It was she who'd supplied most of the evidence for the case. In the attorney general's temporary office, set up in a downtown hotel room, she'd worked as tirelessly for the State of Michigan as she'd once worked for the Seventh Kingdom. And yet everything she'd done had merely led up to this moment.

A hush hung over the courtroom as she walked up the aisle and took the oath—a trim little woman of 37 now, still pert and pretty. The rows of long-haired Flying Rollers stared curiously at her. In the years that had gone by since she'd left Benton Harbor, she'd become a legend among the Israelites—a dark sinister menace waiting in the outside world. The newspapers had dubbed her "King Ben's Nemesis," but among the bearded cultists she'd been painted as an evil demon, as the earthly representative of the Prince of Darkness. The Israelites who'd never seen her before were obviously shocked. She certainly looked harmless enough.

The moment she began her testimony, the illusion vanished. Esther was far from harmless.

Except when she told of her seduction aboard the *Rising Sun*, there was very little emotion in this woman's voice as she gave her answers, not even anger. Instead, calm and deadly and efficient, she dealt only in facts and figures. In running through her 18 years as an Israelite, she seemed to know exactly what aspects of King Ben's rule were criminal and she stuck to the important points—his debauching of young girls, his taking money under false pretenses, his defrauding the government by faking dependency records for Israelite draftees, the cases of death and starvation that came from his rule, his blackmail, his forcing his subjects to commit perjury, even his falsifying property-owner records to enable his subjects to vote against school taxes. Most damaging of all, she introduced office records and correspondence and Israelite pamphlets to document nearly everything she had to say.

For three straight days, she piled up a mountain of evidence against Benjamin Franklin Purnell. And on the morning of her fourth day on the witness stand, as she waited for what should have been a feared and dreaded ordeal—the grueling relentless cross-examination that superbly skilled Bill Barnard was sure to give her—a strange out-of-place smile was on her face. It wasn't a smile of nervousness. It was a smile of eagerness, of anticipation. An astounded whisper ran through the press section.

"That woman's actually enjoying this!"

Fifteen

FOR THREE MORE DAYS, six steady hours a day, the great criminal lawyer pounded away unmercifully at the former harem girl, as though he were certain his entire defense depended on shaking her testimony. And as the battle of shouted words raged on, the crowded courtroom watched and listened in startled disbelief. Esther was proving more than a match for the famed attorney. Far from having her direct testimony shaken, she was skillfully taking every opportunity to make new damaging statements about King Ben Purnell.

"Isn't it true," Barnard shouted at her, "that for the last six months the State of Michigan has been paying you to go all over the country to round up witnesses?"

"My expenses were paid!" she shouted right back. "What was I supposed to do—borrow one of King Ben's covered wagons?"

"But you were paid!"

"Even expense money was more than I got when I was fourteen, when I was traveling the country to round up suckers for—"

"These so-called escape tunnels you've described," he broke in. "Isn't it—"

"The tunnels were dug during the Fortney suit of nineteen-fourteen," she broke in, too. "Would you like the names of the men who worked on them or the office records of their work assignments?"

"You save your speech until I finish a question!" he exploded.

"I'll interrupt you just as often as you interrupt me!"

"Isn't it true that those tunnels never really existed?"

"I can show you where they were."

"All right!" He waved his finger in her face. "All right! You'll be given the opportunity of taking us all out to the House of David and leading us through the tunnels."

"I said where they were!" She shoved his hand aside. "They were filled up with dirt in a hurry during the spring of nineteen-twenty-three and I think you know it."

"Your quarrel with Benjamin began over money, didn't it?"

"Money was involved in most quarrels Benjamin had."

Hour after hour, this verbal fencing went on, with the former harem girl more than holding her own and thoroughly enjoying the clash. Again and again, her responses drew cheers from the tightly packed courtroom. But when Judge Louis Fead finally adjourned for the day, a respectful silence followed her as she left the witness chair and walked out down the aisle. Here, in a way, was a crime far more serious than the wholesale debauching of teen-agers. Here was a woman of obvious brilliance whose education had ended at the age of 12, who'd been schooled only in treachery and deceit and insane theology through the vital years that had followed. What Esther Johnson might have achieved, given a normal life, no one would ever know. One thing was certain—she would have been a great trial lawyer.

The second day of her cross-examination turned into a debate over Israelite liturgy, with William Barnard attempting to put only a symbolic interpretation on the various Sacred Writings and Esther offering one example after another to prove King Ben interpreted them literally.

"When Benjamin wrote that his followers should imagine themselves in the presence of Christ when in his presence, didn't he really mean that all Christians should have this constant awareness of Christ and conduct themselves accordingly?"

"Absolutely not. He meant that he was a second Christ, another Messiah—no more and no less!"

After many hours of this, not only the courtroom audience but even Judge Fead became bored.

"I'm sure you've pretty well exhausted this line of questioning, Counselor," he told Barnard. "I'll adjourn for the day now. And if you intend continuing this cross-examination in the morning, I'd suggest you move on to a more pertinent subject."

Esther Johnson's sixth day in the witness chair began very much like her fourth, with Bill Barnard even covering a good deal of the same ground as he fought futilely to trip the woman up, to trick her into answers inconsistent with her earlier testimony.

"You've stated that during the war Benjamin encouraged his followers to become conscientious objectors. Isn't it true . . "

"I said ordered, not encouraged."

"Isn't it true that he was merely advocating peace in the world, that he was fanatically devoted to peace, that he was always by nature a peaceful man and . . ."

"Hardly. He carried a revolver at all times after the Harry Williams trouble in nineteen-eight. He kept leaded billy-clubs in a locker in the main office. He hit me with his fist and knocked me down once when he was in a rage over the Pritchard charges. He constantly referred to all outsiders, Gentiles and Jews alike as swine. He . . ."

When the state's attorneys began objecting to the endless repetition, the defense lawyer turned his frustrated rage on the prosecution table, actually challenging the attorney general and his entire staff to step outside with him, offering to take them on one at a time or all together. Promptly reprimanded by Judge Fead for his antics, he came very close to a contempt citation.

"Your honor, I demand that you . . ."

"You don't demand anything in my courtroom!" Judge Fead retorted. I'd like to remind you that there is no jury here, that I alone will be deciding the issue here. You will go just as far as I allow you to go and no further. Now proceed with your questioning!"

"Whatever his fee, Bill Barnard was earning it. He refused to give up, no matter how hopeless the fight had become. Hour after hour he thundered at Esther. Hour after hour, she answered every question instantly and continued to slip in new adverse evidence at every opportunity.

Then suddenly and unexpectedly, after six long days in the witness chair, she collapsed completely. Judge Fead recessed court and called for a doctor to examine the sick, choking and exhausted woman. When the doctor ordered her sent to a hospital, the former harem girl fought the attendants who tried to help her down the aisle.

"I want to go back there!" Esther shouted, pointing at the witness stand. "I haven't even started yet! I've got a lot more to tell about that . . ."

When the trial resumed, two former Israelites testified —Richard Adkins, who'd worked on the escape tunnels; and Richard T. Wade, still wearing the wide-brimmed hat he'd worn in his Wichita days. On June 6, the state called another woman to the stand, the former Gladys Hill, the childhood sweetheart Ben Purnell had taken away from his own son Coy.

"How old were you when you entered the colony?"

"Just thirteen."

"What work assignment was given you?"

"I was the House of David schoolteacher."

"At the age of thirteen? How far had your own education progressed?"

"I'd been through the first half of the eighth grade in Canada."

"Were you allowed to continue your own education?"

"No. I cried all night when I found out I couldn't finish the eighth grade."

"Were you able to teach the children to read and write?"

"I wasn't supposed to. I just read the Sacred Writings aloud to them."

"Then the colony children were raised in complete illiteracy?"

"Yes."

"Were you forced to submit to blood-cleansing rites?"

"Yes, when I was fifteen. King Benjamin called me and a girl named Violet Tucker into his office one evening when no one else was there and locked the door."

Gladys was silent for a long time. Then she suddenly rose to her feet and pointed at the center of the row of long-haired Israelites behind the defense-counsel table.

"And I told my sister-in-law—Rosie Plank Hill, sitting right there—all about it! And she wouldn't do anything! She said everything King Benjamin did was all right!"

"Is it true," George Nichols asked when he'd calmed her, "that King Ben deliberately destroyed your friendship with his son Coy?"

"It wasn't just a friendship!" Gladys sobbed. "I loved him. I really loved him. Everyone said it was on account of the Fortney trouble that he left the colony. But that wasn't it. It was because his father put me in Shiloh with all the rest. That was the real reason."

Mrs. Isabelle Pritchard, the Australian widow, told her story next. And then the State of Michigan called its second star witness to the stand—the former Hazel Ruth Wade, now divorced from her Israelite husband and happy in a real marriage, but still willing to come out of obscurity and risk notoriety to testify against the man who'd destroyed her family and ruined her early life.

The older Flying Rollers in the courtroom audience, who'd been charmed by Salvation Nell in the years when she was the darling of the House of David, saw a very different person take the witness chair now. The long brown ringlets that had given her a doll-like look in her evangelist days were gone; her hair had been bobbed. But her voice was still warm and husky, appealingly sad. In her mid-thirties now, she was still a very beautiful woman.

Where Esther Johnson's testimony had been sharp

and factual, Hazel Ruth's was unabashedly emotional, but it was every bit as effective, even in a non-jury trial where only a veteran judge would decide the case. In her own soft-throated words, with the prosecutor interjecting his brief questions as seldom as possible, she told the pathetic story of her dozen years at the House of David—the breakup of her family, her forced and brutal initiation into the Inner Circle, the strange pattern of her life when she'd alternated missionary duty with duty in the second-floor rooms of Shiloh, her mother's death, her forced marriage to Irving Smith, the unbelievable story of how the man who'd debauched her had heatedly condemned her for kissing her legal husband on the cheek, her awakening in the outside world, her return to rescue her sister, and finally, her fruitless trip to Washington to ask President Wilson's help.

Throughout the full day she took in telling her story, the courtroom was almost completely silent. Not one of the case-hardened veteran trial reporters in the press section thought for a moment of doubting a thing she said. It had to be true, all of it. The human imagination was simply incapable of creating such a tale.

Her cross-examination also took a full day. In sharp contrast to Esther Johnson, she seemed timid, almost apologetic. Even so, in spite of the fact that the defense lawyer attacked her just as belligerently as he had Esther, her testimony remained unshaken.

"Do you remember a man named Marston?" William Barnard demanded. "A convert you brought back to the House of David in your covered wagon?"

Hazel Ruth shook her head. "I brought back a great many converts."

"What would you say if I told you I have a written affidavit from Mr. Marston, an affidavit swearing that he had intimate relations with you during that trip?"

"I'd say it was typical enough of the way King Benjamin defends himself. It sounds exactly like the methods he used to discredit the Fortney girls in nineteen-fourteen. Most of us gave false statements for him at one time or another. We were taught he had a Divine right to ask this of us."

"You've stated that the House of David is an immoral place and should be abolished. Now forget Benjamin for just a moment. Did you ever seen any immoral acts committed by anyone else in the colony?"

"Yes," she told him. "Mary Purnell and Francis Thorpe."

"Oh, come now!"

"And Cora Mooney, who beat little Eliza Murphy half to death with a razor strop for telling her mother what Benjamin had done to her. Eliza was banished to High Island soon afterward and she killed herself by drinking poison there. Another girl, Jessie Wheeler, tried the same thing on the island, but she didn't drink enough. She was sick for a long long time, though."

In spite of what seemed timidity in her voice, Hazel Ruth's story could not be dented or qualified in the slightest. Bill Barnard made a futile hour-long attempt to trap her by bringing out the blueprints of Shiloh and asking her to define the harem quarters, then loudly demanding to know how the house could possibly hold so many girls. She told him, describing the tiers of bunks, and he finally gave up on her.

Hazel Ruth Wade stepped down from the witness stand and walked swiftly out of the courtroom, back to her husband and the new life she'd built for herself. The country's newspapers would carry her testimony in full detail in the morning, just as they'd done in 1923. But this was the last time. For her, the nightmare story that had begun when her mother had browsed too long in an Israelite exhibit at the St. Louis World's Fair was finally finished.

On and on, in a steady seemingly endless string, the former harem girls came like ghosts from Ben Purnell's past, each adding a few new strands to the already incontrovertible web of evidence the State of Michigan had woven about him.

"When I finally got up enough nerve to tell my mother, she made me swear it on the Bible," Hilda Pritchard testified. "Then she dragged me along with her when she went looking for him."

"I was just fourteen the first time he took me into Shiloh," her sister Irene remembered. "It was right after a service at the Tabernacle, right after he'd finished preaching."

"Whenever anyone died, it meant they'd been evil," Dorothy Wade said. "When our mother died she had to be quarantined for a week, so no one would catch the evil. A girl I knew was publicly ostracized for a long time for touching her father's body."

"We turned in everything, even my wedding ring," Mrs. Eliza Bamford, who'd decided to join her daughters and tell the truth now, related. "I had to go through his blood-cleansing rites from the beginning. But even so, I still couldn't believe it when my girls first told me. My God, Ruth was born there! King Benjamin saw her the day she was born and knew her ever since she was a baby. She was only fourteen then. I just couldn't believe it. How could he do such a thing!"

"Queen Mary kept insisting I had to pick out a boy's name and be married," Ruth Bamford testified. "So I finally said, 'All right, Francis Thorpe!' Her face got red and she left me alone after that."

"I heard someone screaming and I ran to the door," Gladys Bamford told the court. "Just as I got there, Cora Mooney was coming out with the razor strap. I asked what was the matter. She said, 'Eliza Murphy has been telling lies about Benjamin again!'"

"The first time he tried it I fought him off and kicked him in the stomach," the former Ione Smith testified. "And he just laughed. He said I'd end up coming to him. After that no one would speak to me. Not one of the girls I'd played with—no one at all. Wherever I went, everyone would look the other way. I was only fourteen and I couldn't stand it when everyone called me a scorpion. I finally decided nothing could be as bad as that, and I went to him, just like he said I would."

"I worked ten years in the colony," Emil Rosetti said. "When I left I got ten dollars. I got a dollar a year."

"Esther Johnson and I censored all mail," Edith Meldrum informed the court. "Out-going and in-coming too."

"In seventeen years at the House of David," her mother mentioned, "I was given about fifteen-dollar's-worth of clothing."

"Sometimes he read the Sacred Writings to us in the evening," Estelle Mills related. "And sometimes he read dirty stories and laughed like a madman."

"My husband thought it was my fault," Edith Clark remembered. "But just living in that place, you got so you thought that everything King Benjamin did had to be right and the most evil thing you could do was disobey him."

"Half the people in the colony told lies about us and swore to it in court," Augusta Fortney testified.

"If a woman turned up pregnant, even a married woman, she was thrown out of the colony for breaking the Virgin Law," Etidorpha Moore related. "But I wasn't when Marie was born, because King Benjamin knew it was really his child. So he called it a virgin birth and said she was the "Sunshine Child" and passed her off as a Divine visitation."

Defense attorney Barnard, who'd been fighting a steadily losing battle, decided to challenge this.

"Your daughter has red-gold hair, hasn't she? And both you and your husband have red-gold hair. And Benjamin Purnell's hair was black. Now are you really trying to tell us . . ."

"Benjamin's hair was the same color as Marie's is now. He just dyed it black. Everyone knows that."

On June 22, the State of Michigan finally called its last witness. Bessie Daniels, the girl who'd led the police to his hiding place, told of the last years of his reign—just as Angelina had told of his earliest known years on the first day of testimony. The prosecution then rested.

William Barnard had promised the press that for every

former Israelite who testified against Ben Purnell, a half-dozen witnesses would be produced to swear he was a living saint, and he made good that promise. He opened his defense by once again characterizing all of the charges as a vast plot hatched up by apostate cultists who'd been expelled from the colony because they were unable to live up to the high moral standards King Benjamin demanded of them, cultists who now hoped to share in the proceeds if the kingdom was abolished. He introduced a long petition from Benton Harbor citizens opposing the abolishing of the colony. He vigorously attacked the prosecution, the police and the newspapers. Then he began calling an endless procession of Flying Rollers to the stand.

The Little People of the sect made good witnesses, for most of them actually believed what they were saying. Every trick Ben Purnell had learned in his quarter-century reign was brought forth to save his kingdom now. His subjects perjured themselves both on the stand and in written statements in attempts to discredit the girls who'd aided the prosecution.

But it was all futile. The case had actually been lost when Esther Johnson's exact and detailed testimony had held up under three days' cross-examination, when Hazel Ruth Wade's pathetic story had remained unshaken. Late in August, Judge Fead adjourned the case. On December 5, after months of studying the 15,000-page transcript, he handed down a 191-page decision.

The House of David was to be abolished as a menace to public morals.

Successful in this, the State of Michigan prepared to prosecute Ben Purnell on the three charges of rape that were pending. But in spite of the magnitude of the case against him, the long-haired prophet escaped earthly punishment. The Israelite attorneys produced sworn statements from his doctors that he had only a short time to live, and he was allowed to return to the colony —accompanied by an injunction prohibiting him from having anything at all to do with the young girls of the cult.

Even on his deathbed, the court didn't trust him.

"What will happen when he dies?" newsmen asked Judge DeWhirst.

"Benjamin cannot die!" the long-haired Pillar insisted.

"That isn't what his doctors say. As a matter of fact, that isn't what you argued in court."

"Render unto Caesar the things that are Caesar's. Doctors have their medical books. Courts have their law books. We of the True Faith have our Sacred Writings. And they tell us the Seventh Messenger cannot die."

"But just suppose he did," the reporters persisted. "Then what?"

"If he were to die, it would mean he was not the Seventh Messenger. The Sacred Writings say there will be such a Messenger."

On December 16, 1927, Benjamin Franklin Purnell's breathing became extremely spasmodic and his pulse began failing.

"I am merely going away for a while," he whispered to the grieving Pillars. "The blood that was given to me for mortal life, for purifying and granting immortality to others, I will no longer need. It will be hardened to solid flesh for the new life to come. I will return in exactly four days and the Millennium will begin. So be ye ready!"

He called Queen Mary to him.

"I never really believed you were guilty of any carnal sin with your Little Lamb," he told her. "But if you were, I absolve you of it."

A few minutes later his breathing ended in a fit of choking.

The Israelites joyfully and confidently announced to the world that he'd rise from the dead in exactly 96 hours. The county coroner matter-of-factly announced to the Israelites that state law required the embalming of a body within 72 hours. And Judge DeWhirst made a frantic appeal to the courts.

"Give us the fourth day!" he pleaded.

A special court order was issued, setting aside the law, giving the corpse every conceivable chance. A gigantic army of reporters joined in the vigil, camping on the very steps of Diamond House. But when the specified time passed with no sign of life in the clever old fraud, who even in death seemed to be secretly laughing at those who worshipped him, the newsmen went on to other assignments and the world forgot King Ben, leaving the bearded cultists to wait for his resurrection in silence and obscurity.

And there in Benton Harbor, Michigan—even today—a few of them are still waiting.

Epilogue

THE LOGS of the Roundhouse Harem Shack on High Island have rotted back into the earth from which they grew, and the Israelite colony at Benton Harbor is slowly melting back into the society that spawned it. Not once, since the death of Benjamin Franklin Purnell, has the slighest hint of scandal come to the House of David.

When the resurrection attempt failed, Judge H. T. DeWhirst immediately began a long hard fight to have the decision to abolish the colony reversed by the higher courts. Expertly and eloquently, he argued that many of the Little People would be helpless in the outside world. On June 3, 1929, the Michigan Supreme Court handed down its decision. It stated that Judge Fead's ruling had been the proper one, that there could be no reasonable doubt of King Ben's guilt. But it also stated that abolishing the colony as a menace to public morals was no longer necessary. A Higher Power had abolished the real menace.

Then a full-scale fight for control of the ten-million-dollar kingdom exploded. The attorney general ventured the opinion that Ben's legal wife Angelina was the correct heir, and for a time it seemed that the little old mountain lady would inherit the vast fortune. But Judge DeWhirst managed to block this in the courts, arguing that the Israelite property should remain with those who'd donated it and multiplied it with their labor.

Queen Mary suddenly realized that DeWhirst was becoming increasingly powerful in the cult. With the help of Francis Thorpe, she tried to oust him. Instead, she found herself ousted. The office staff, the key Pillars—all were loyal to DeWhirst. Of the 500 Israelites who remained in the colony, no more than 200 supported Mary Purnell. She went into court in an attempt to regain control, but she was no match for the former judge there. In 1930 she finally accepted an outside settlement, receiving a hotel and some farmland and an undisclosed but not too sizable share of the cash in Ben's vaults. She led her followers out of the original colony, building a new set of smaller cheaper dwellings such a short distance down the road that most tourists think of both colonies as a single community.

Calling themselves "The Israelite House of David as Re-Organized by Mary Purnell," the Queen's followers have kept alive the Flying Roller religion, developing among themselves the fiction that Mary was the co-author of Ben's Sacred Writings, more or less raising her to Divine status. She invested a good share of the settlement she received in a radio station and a sewage disposal plant, and her group soon became comfortably well off.

But it was the DeWhirst faction that prospered most sensationally. With the ball team and the park as going enterprises, the judge invested in a wide variety of concerns—a giant fruit-canning plant, greenhouses, a 72-unit motel, a service station, a used car lot, even a fine night club complete with a floor show and a long-haired bearded jazz band. When DeWhirst died in October of 1947, his followers had an income of well over a million a year.

Neither group has encouraged converts in recent years. Both are growing steadily smaller, with no young people among them. Within a decade or so, the strange twisted story begun some 168 years ago by an English scrubwoman will fade to its anticlimactic ending.

Mary Purnell lived to the age of 91, passing away in August of 1953.

"Sister Mary will be raised immortal!" an Israelite woman sobbed to the handful of reporters who covered the occasion. "She taught us life, not death!"

"No one can ever take her place!" a white-bearded long-haired Pillar agreed.

The Little People of the sect were silent, just as they'd
been silent while their king was making headlines, just
as they'd been silent when his harem girls had come back
in anger to topple him. They went on leading the only
life they knew, waiting for the only thing that held
meaning for them—the Millennium, the time of rest and
reward.

But when they hope for the man who originally rallied
them at Benton Harbor to rise from the dead and lead
them again, they must look down the street to the colony
of the hated DeWhirst adherents, the wordly "Danites"
who are more interested in making money than preserv-
ing the True Faith. For they have the prophet's body,
still enshrined at Diamond House.

Benjamin Franklin Purnell is in remarkably good con-
dition, for a $13,000 preserving job was done on his
body by a St. Louis man who claimed to have discovered
and improved upon ancient Egyptian methods. His
hands are clasped across his chest. A baby-pink ribbon
is tied in his long white hair. Embalming fluid has been
in his veins for 32 years, but his eyes still seem to be
smiling.

—The End—

www.ingramcontent.com/pod-product-compliance
Lightning Source LLC
Chambersburg PA
CBHW071951150726

47999CB00001B/404